RONARO

THE
MIRACLE
KNOWN AS
ED LEVINE
BASED ON A TRUE STORY

White Station
PUBLISHING, LLC

DEDICATIONS

I dedicate this book to Rona Train for telling my story, and to both Rona and her husband L.A. for always being there for me. I feel it is imperative to also include the entire Train family for all the support they have given me. Without them, there would have been no tomorrows for me and no story to tell.

The real Ed Levine

I dedicate my work to L.A. Train, who encourages me in all ways, and to my family and friends for their support. Ed and Linda continue to inspire me, and I am grateful and humbled by their trust.

Ronarose Train

INTRODUCTION

"Stage four. Get your affairs in order, Ed."

Lung cancer had met its match.

My friend Ed Levine is a fighter. Against prejudice and discrimination. Poverty. War. Dyslexia. Cancer. He is a living miracle. His courage and determination so inspired me that I was compelled to write his story. Names, places, and industries are necessarily fictitious, though events are based on fact.

Ed and I developed a greater bond as we delved into his history, each of us learning from and appreciating the other. It was, is my honor to chronicle this remarkable man's journey.

Ed Levine's affairs have been in order for seventeen years...and still counting.

Ronarose Train

PART ONE
ONE

EAST END

World War II did not pause on August 19, 1942, for the birth of Ed Levine. Ambulances and cars in London were scarce, only used for emergencies, and were rarely seen. Wounded soldiers filled the few hospitals still standing, forcing civilians to search for any makeshift clinic they could find. Consequently, Ed's parents kept a constant record of locations accepting women in labor.

"Oy, Max! It's coming soon."

"We have to leave right away," he said, wrapping Miriam in a shawl and picking up the bag they had prepared.

"Don't walk so fast," his wife pleaded. "I don't see the bus yet."

"It's at the corner," Max said after they had queued only a short time.

He carefully helped her up the stairs of the crowded double-decker and thanked the man who offered Miriam his seat.

Before long, her cries joined those of the many laboring mothers lying on the stretchers that lined the poorly equipped medical facility's halls. Bomb explosions added to the chaos.

Miriam saw the conditions around her. "Everyone is so busy," she said to the woman on the next cot. "And there aren't many nurses."

"Most of them are taking care of soldiers," she said to Miriam. "We can't worry. Someone will come."

"But that woman has been lying there with her baby on her chest since I got here. I think the umbilical cord is still attached."

"He's healthy, so what's the hurry?"

Miriam lowered her voice. "Have you noticed that all of us in this hall are Jews?"

"So?"

"Is that why they aren't helping us?"

"When yours is ready, you don't need anyone. I've seen two already."

Miriam writhed in pain, and between contractions, returned to her new friend's remark. "Two what?"

"Births without help," the woman said. "Not even a midwife."

"Oy. Why am I having this baby?" Miriam lamented.

"It's too late to ask that," her friend said.

Accompanied by occasional warning sirens and explosions, Ed Levine made a howling entry into this world at 3:00 p.m. The chimes emanating from the East End's Mary-le-Bow church heralded his arrival. Those in earshot of the hourly "Bow Bell" concerts proudly claimed their heritage: they were Cockneys, the rugged inhabitants of London's factory and warehouse district, the area vital to England's war effort, and a target of relentless Nazi bombing.

The East End was London's immigrant section where housing was cheap, and ethnic hatred ran deep. Even though they faced anti-Semitism in London, the Levines believed they were better off there than facing the Communism spreading across Eastern Europe. They led a poor, hard-working life among East Enders of similar means, and all endured the constant hardship of war.

Eddie, their fourth child, would join a family of much older siblings. Twenty-one-year-old Sidney was serving his country in India and Burma. Fifteen-year-old Trudy lived at home with her parents and worked as a manicurist at nearby Bobbington Air Base. In response to Winston Churchill's effort to send young British children away from danger, seven-year-old Joan became one of the almost 900,000 school-age evacuees separated from their families. She lived in the Scottish countryside with a willing family of farmers, who would adopt her if her parents did not survive the war.

Eddie's three uncles served in the military. British practice prohibited the youngest brother, Eddie's father, Max, from enlisting, thus allowing the family at least one surviving breadwinner. The country needed all able men, however, and he did his part as a civilian policeman, supplementing the low pay by continuing to barber. Unwilling to join his brothers in a business and risk losing money, at the age of fifteen, he had apprenticed to the five-year barber training program, reasoning that it was a respected and steady vocation. He was proud of his accomplishment as a successful barber, who was so skilled he was able to work in the wealthy West End's finest hotel shops.

As a civilian policeman during the war, Max received less than the small salary he had earned as a barber. He earned tips in this temporary profession, not in coins but with a cuppa— the Cockney word for a cup of tea—or maybe an apple. He supplemented by cutting hair at Bobbington Air Base. Charged with monitoring his neighborhood in any way necessary, Eddie's father checked bombed buildings for trapped people, helped to clear rubble, and watched out for criminal activity.

British civilian police didn't carry guns. Instead, they learned to put a culprit out of action by hitting his shoulder with a truncheon, the short, stout batons British Bobbies carried. Even after his war service, Max kept the truncheon hanging from his bedpost, ready to defend his family. A friendly guy, he did his job with dignity and compassion. A criminal was fortunate if Eddie's father was the understanding copper who caught him.

London's East End residents endured incessant bombing, increasing shortages, and fear. They prayed to survive, learning that things here today could very well be gone tomorrow. Like buildings. Like neighbors. Max and Miriam Levine's fourth child faced a perilous world.

TWO

Miriam sensed them before she heard them. "Hurry, Trudy. The sirens!"

Home instead of working that day, sixteen-year-old Trudy ceased sweeping the living room of the small East End home and ran to the tiny bedroom she shared with eight-month-old Eddie. She picked up her sleeping brother and his blanket and said, "Don't cry, Eddie. We're going to the tube. You can sleep there."

"Trudy, I can hold him. You carry our gas masks." Miriam turned off their evening dinner simmering on the stove, wrapped her son in the blanket, and took him in her arms. They hurried to the closest entrance to the tube, the subway system of trains that traversed greater London. They joined neighbors running to the stairways leading to the underground tunnels. Women, children, and old men sought safety and prayed that their military would soon defeat the evil enemy.

"Do you see them?" someone asked as Miriam glanced upward, scanning the skies for Nazi bombers.

"No, but they're coming."

"Hurry," a woman urged no one in particular. "The sirens are always right."

"The buzzing comes first, but all I hear are frightened people," a man said.

The sense of urgency spread as throngs of people rushed to safety. Miriam and Trudy descended several long flights of stairs and maneuvered through the closely packed crowd, everyone seeking positions underground. They stepped over outstretched legs and sleeping babies, searching for a comfortable spot among the hundreds of people already sheltering.

Nora Greenberg called out, "There's room by me, Miriam. Sit here. We can lean against the wall and stretch out our legs. My son is working with his grandfather today, so we have room."

"You're a blessing, Nora. If it's okay with you, Eddie can nap on both of our laps, and we can talk until the all-clear."

Settling into the cramped territory between families, Nora pulled her coat closed and adjusted her knit hat to cover her ears. "Do you want to borrow one of my gloves?"

"Thanks. I gave mine to Trudy." Miriam looked around as she pulled on the glove. "Did you see where she went?" she asked, realizing her independent third-born had disappeared.

"She's over there. Isn't that her mate Kathleen?"

Miriam shouted to her daughter. "Trudy, you can stay with the Finebergs if you want, as long as I can still see you. Don't lose your gas mask." Her daughter waved and sat on the floor with her friend.

Comfortably cushioned on the ample laps of the two mothers, the toddler resumed his nap while the women voiced their usual complaints. "How much longer can this last?"

"Didn't Churchill promise it would end quickly now?" asked Miriam.

"That was when the Americans came into it."

"It's been three years." Nodding their heads in resignation, the friends huddled for warmth. They talked about their precarious existence and the repeated escapes to the underground. "It's a miracle we're still alive, Nora. Are we really safe in these old tunnels?"

"I pray that we are, but if a bomb hits the buildings just above us, we're going to die...and it won't be so nice."

"You're right, I'm sure. Don't you hate it down here?"

"It stinks. Like the loo. Like unwashed bodies. Like fear." They listened to the noises above. "Did you hear that, Miriam? They're close now."

"The buzzing is so loud! They must be right above us." People screamed as they dodged falling plaster and tiles. Mothers stifled their sobs as they held their wailing children close to their breasts.

As the dust and noise settled, the crowd assessed the damage, then tended to the wounded and hysterical around them. Miriam held her frightened son and looked for her daughter. Trudy was holding a baby while Mrs. Fineberg spoke to its shaking mother. Miriam called out over the din, "Come to me, *bubila*. When you can."

After handing the child to its calmer mother, Trudy made her way to Miriam. "The lady was so upset that she almost smothered her baby."

Miriam hugged her daughter. "You were very brave to help."

"I was scared, too. The noise hurt my ears, but the baby was more frightened than me."

When there was a lull in the action, the old men dozed or spoke to each other about the last Great War. They had accomplished nothing. Finally, the all-clear sounded, and the crowd returned to their neighborhoods and factories to inspect the damage. Constant bombings were wearing down the nerves but not the will of the British people.

When warnings again sent them underground, those sheltering in the tunnels discussed their fate. What would a family do if their home were hit? How could a returning soldier find a job if his former employer no longer had a factory? The helter-skelter piles of broken masonry and debris interspersed with sections of inhabitable buildings were now a reality, and the rubble increased as bombs fell. East Enders endured hours of uncertainty day after day, braced for the daunting conditions they would find above ground.

"It looks like only a few are hurt," Miriam said as the sirens finally indicated the danger was over for now. She noticed a woman tearing her slip. "Hold Eddie, please," she said to Nora, then went to the woman. "Let me help." Miriam took the strip of material from the stranger and used it to wrap her arm. "That should stop the bleeding until you get home."

"Thank you," the woman said. "I'm lucky." She pointed. "That lady is nursing a broken arm."

A woman who had overheard her comment said, "It was the brick ceiling. I saw a section fall."

"So, a broken arm isn't so bad," Miriam commented.

"Sure. Could have hit her head." The women shuddered, realizing such a thing could happen to anyone trapped in the old tunnels.

"We have to help each other, don't we?" Nora said when Miriam rejoined her. "Everyone's terrified!"

"It's dangerous down here, too," Miriam said. "Sometimes, I think we should just crawl under our beds and wait. If a bomb finds me, then at least it will be over quickly."

"And it probably smells a lot better under your bed than it does down here," Nora said, laughing as they moved toward the stairs with the sea of people.

Miriam cautioned a man who was pushing his way through the packed crowd streaming to the exits. "No need to hurry. We'll all get home if we're patient."

"You mean if there's a home to get to," Nora said. "And if it's still standing, we'll be lucky if our doors and windows haven't blown out."

"True," Miriam said as she turned to look at her friend. "Really. I'm always surprised to see that our house is still there."

Nora nodded. "Me, too. They're small, but they're home."

The friends walked the two blocks and said good-bye at the Levine's front step. Both entered their houses, grateful to be resuming their lives with roofs over their heads. After a respite of two hours, the sirens again sounded. Miriam gathered her children to return to the tunnels.

"Miriam!" Nora, just leaving her house, yelled to her neighbor. "Wait for me."

"I'm so tired of this, Nora. I wish we could just go back to the way things were. Be everyday homemakers, maybe have a cup of tea. Talk about our neighbors."

Each considered the audacious proposal. "We could just as easily be killed in the tunnels," Nora said. "I'd rather die comfortably at home." She chuckled weakly.

"Why don't we stay here?" Miriam ventured.

In simultaneous agreement, they said, "Why not?"

The ladies returned to the Levine kitchen, gossiping and watching Trudy encourage her brother as Eddie repeatedly put spoons into pots and then dumped them out.

When the sound of buzzing indicated a dropping bomb, Miriam held her squirming son close, and Nora shielded Trudy as they crowded together under the kitchen table. Each time the repeated explosions subsided, the friends amiably sipped tea and chatted in the comfort of a home. That is, until the next buzz sent them back to their sanctuary.

"That one had to be very close," they agreed as dishes and windows rattled, and pictures tumbled to the floor.

They braced for another rumble but felt nothing. A siren finally sounded through the silence.

"There's the all-clear," Nora said. "This was such a better way to shelter!" She took her leave.

In seconds, she returned.

Her face was ashen, and her voice trembled as she said, "It's not there! Our house. It's just gone!" Both women collapsed into a fierce hug and sobbed, Miriam's tears as hysterical as her friend's.

It had been a direct hit on Nora's home. All that remained was a single lead pipe that protruded from the ground, Nora's porcelain sink still attached. In the sink were a dozen eggs that she had bought on the black market to share with friends. Not a single one was broken.

Thankfully, the women had chosen the Levine family's kitchen rather than Nora's, and it was only a building that had been lost. But the friends had learned their lesson, and thereafter gratefully returned to the tube.

THREE

Training new air crews during World War II was a massive program that required several sites. Located just miles from the Levine's neighborhood, Bobbington Air Base construction began in 1940 and was completed a year later. The base included seven steel hangars, several technical buildings, many mess halls, Post Exchange facilities, and living quarters. Throughout the war, it was used for the continual training of British, Canadian, Free French, Australian, New Zealand, and American airmen. Hundreds of seasoned pilots flew reconnaissance and bombing missions out of Bobbington.

When Eddie's father Max suffered acute ulceritis in 1943, the police department discharged him from wartime service. After his recovery, he returned to barbering, this time at Bobbington. The pilots liked weekly haircuts and manicures, and the Americans and Canadians could afford a shave as well.

Eddie's sister Trudy, had trained for five years to obtain her manicurist license and now worked along with her father. One particularly insistent mechanic flirted with her during his haircuts, manicures, and shaves. He finally gathered the nerve to ask her out on a date.

"I'll have to ask my father," she said.

"Who's your father?"

"He's the one with the razor at your throat right now."

The smitten young man received permission, and eventually, Trudy's hand in marriage as well.

As the war escalated, Bobbington activity focused on military missions. "Aren't you going to the base today?" Miriam asked her husband one day. "This is the second time this week you haven't put on your fedora and kissed me good-bye."

"No point in it," he said. "I only had two customers yesterday. Just haircuts and no shaves. The pilots are flying missions around the clock, and all support personnel are on duty. The planes must be maintained and loaded with bombs. No time for a barber when freedom is at stake."

"At least Trudy is busy. It doesn't hurt that those lonely guys are hungry to spend a few minutes with a beautiful girl. We need every bob she earns."

"I'll spend some time tending our fruit trees," Max said. "We have to grow as much as possible from our allotment. Maybe we'll be allowed to keep the chickens."

The war took two of Eddie's older siblings away from home, and Trudy rarely had the time or inclination to pay attention to him. Surrounded by anti-Semitic Christian neighbors, who didn't allow their children to play with the Jewish boy, young Eddie learned to be alone. Deprived of companionship, by the age of three, he had developed an acceptable alternative. His playmates lived behind their house.

"Chickie, chickie," Eddie said as every day, he sprinkled corn and watched with delight as the chickens devoured it. Even before the war, his mother, Miriam, had raised chickens to supplement the family's food purchases. It was now illegal to keep them without proper authorization, which would have been denied even if she had applied for it. The war took farmers from their fields and into battle, reducing production and drastically curtailing food availability for the civilian population. Britain's top priorities had to be the military, creating a serious shortage throughout the country.

"You have chickens?" asked the solemn man in the drab civilian policeman uniform.

Miriam hesitated. The truth was not the right answer. "Why do you want to know?"

"Here's the report," he said, showing her the form. "We have to feed our soldiers. We know you have chickens."

Eddie began to cry as he followed his mother and the man to the small enclosure outside.

"Mrs. Sullivan, that *mamser*," Miriam said as she noticed her neighbor watching the spectacle.

"No! No!" Eddie screamed, hitting the man's legs while he put the boy's cackling friends in a crate. "They're mine," he protested long after the van drove away. "Mine."

More concerned with the loss of the family's food, Miriam didn't pamper her son. "Find something else, *boychick*. Right now, we have a war."

The Brits faced shortages that set their way of life back years. Home refrigerators were unavailable in nineteen-forties England, not even for those who were wealthy enough to pay for them. British women spent hours every day shopping for fresh food. Each morning, farmers, fishmongers, and purveyors of meat brought their goods to the shops and outdoor markets around London, where housewives bought their daily provisions. The bombs worsened the shortage, keeping the search for food a constant danger, effort, and worry.

The Levines were dirt poor but no different from anyone else in the East End. The black market offered everything from food and household commodities to cigarettes, but Max's meager earnings couldn't afford the exorbitant prices. His innovative wife learned to stretch one egg with water to feed the entire family. Occasionally, the Levine's larder was so bare that Miriam risked illegal behavior, taking care to employ this desperate tactic only once at any market.

"Excuse me, is this the end?" she asked the last woman standing in a line that extended out of the building.

"Yes, and I hope you're wearing comfortable shoes. I've been here twenty minutes and barely moved three steps."

In the five hours it took to reach the front of the special queue, Miriam got to know the women around her and successfully maintained the ruse that she was one of them. The pillows securely tied under her husband's overcoat left no doubt that she, too, qualified for the scarce produce and occasional culinary delicacies available only to pregnant women. Desperate circumstances dictated desperate measures.

Eddie was too young at the time to understand what was happening in his city. Londoners made their hazardous way to work, to markets, and shelters, picking their routes along bombed-out streets piled with rubble and lined by crumbling walls. They always carried their gas masks and listened for the ominous buzzing of a falling missile.

One day, Max and his daughter Trudy joined the dwindling number of workers carefully navigating their way to the closest remaining stop, hoping a bus would appear. As a former civilian policeman, Max continued to check the condition of the neighborhood each morning as he escorted Trudy to join the group going to Bobbington Air Base. The intrepid bus drivers were forced to find a different route each day, seeking increasingly rare passable roads.

"It's already late," Trudy said to the few men standing with her and Max.

"What else do we have to do?" one neighbor asked. "We can wait a while longer."

Their attention was drawn upward as buzzing interrupted their musing. "Down!" a man's voice cried.

Trudy pulled on her gas mask as someone pushed her onto the street, and she felt the heavy weight of a person on top of her. Her protector remained still while Trudy lay terrified, trying to breathe normally into her mask. "Help!" she yelled several minutes after the explosion noises and dust had subsided. "I can't get up!"

"*Oy gevalt!*" Max exclaimed. "He's dead!" With the help of the stunned survivors, he moved Trudy's lifeless shield, carefully handling the shrapnel-pierced body, and gently laying him on the ground. "Who is he?"

"It's Hannigan's nephew. He was on leave visiting them. Must have been reporting back to Bobbington."

Max held his shaking and dazed daughter while he said Kaddish, the mourner's prayer, honoring the brave soldier who saved his child.

"Come, Trudy, the bus is here. We need to work today."

Though death had become an everyday occurrence, they had to focus on survival. Limited supplies, barely afforded on the few pounds plus tips Eddie's father and sister earned per week, were an ongoing challenge for the parents trying to maintain their home and family during World War II.

Forced to queue patiently for increasingly sparse food, Londoners took what was available rather than what they preferred. After a nine-hour wait one especially crowded day at the Whitecross Market, only a twenty-minute walk away, Miriam ecstatically brought a rare purchase home to her three-year-old son.

"This is a banana," she said. "We haven't had bananas since you were a baby."

The child opened his mouth to experience the new fruit and quickly spit it into his mother's hand. "Ugh! Tastes bad!"

Her stern scowl as she pushed him to a chair facing the corner emphasized the harsh message. "We cannot waste food, Eddie, not after I spend all day waiting and paying dearly for it! Stay there until your father comes home to give you what-for!"

At that young age, Eddie already knew about "what-for." A spanking, a shaking, time in the corner. He learned to avoid his mother's wrath. If those yellow things known as bananas brought on what-for, he'd stay away from them.

Coal was scarce, and people available to deliver it more so. Old men and strong women led the team of massive Clydesdale horses pulling heavily laden carts over bombed roads, and customers bought what they could afford.

Bundled in two sweaters and wool socks, the young Eddie pushed aside the blanket hanging from the kitchen doorway and pulled his mother's hand. "Coalie! Coalie!"

"Thank goodness," Miriam said. "We had just enough for today."

She ordered one sack and took off a glove to gather enough coins from Max's tips as her son stood transfixed, watching the delivery woman shovel the precious fuel into long burlap sacks. Her unique cap was designed for the job, with a leather flap extending down the back from her head to below her waist. For the walk to the coal chute, she bent forward to place the sack on her back, supporting the weight on the leather base. To steady the load, she held the metal rings stitched into the sack's fabric.

The small fireplaces that were set deeply into a wall in every room supplied heat. Several grate-covered holes cut in the outside walls inefficiently carried the toxic coal smoke away. The airborne residue formed a crust on their clothes and every surface in the house, making it impossible to avoid breathing it. It is no wonder that Ed later developed lung cancer.

"Wash your filthy hands," Miriam scolded as she continually attempted to clean their home. Her admonitions did not stop Eddie from drawing pictures in the black dust, repeatedly causing his mother to wash him and his clothes with vigor and frustration.

On winter days, frigid air seeping in through the grates counteracted the warmth of the glowing coal. Families hung blankets or curtains over every doorway to retain heat. Extinguished streetlights kept the neighborhood dark at night to make difficult targets for Nazi bombers, and Max still policed his area to ensure the coverings were enough to black out any sliver of light. However, his biggest job was controlling his mischievous son, who thought moving the coverings to incite his father's stream of colorful language was great fun.

Though the Potsdam Agreement ended the war in 1945, Britain continued to reel from shortages and destruction. Like many parents focused on making ends meet, the Levines allowed their young son to roam freely. Until he enrolled in school at the age of six, his education was the streets. As long as Eddie was home for dinner, Miriam left him to his own devices.

But Fridays were different. The Levine ritual began with a bath in preparation for their special Sabbath dinner. Reluctant to leave his interesting pursuits to face a boring evening, Eddie was often late. "Oy, such dirty hands and face," Miriam said as she handed her tardy son a wet cloth. "You'll have to wash after the Sabbath ends tomorrow night."

"It's not dark yet," four-year-old Eddie said, happy to escape the weekly bath. "Besides, I don't want cholent again." The delicious aroma of fresh bread mingled with the smell of the meat and bean stew.

"G'valt," Miriam said as she spooned his dinner from the simmering pot into a bowl. "I don't know where you go all day. Promise me you'll keep out of trouble."

Eddie slumped as he ignored the stew, and in silence, savored his mother's warm bread, relishing thoughts of the skeletons of buildings he had explored and the apple he had taken when the peddler wasn't looking.

Despite the challenges of war and its aftermath, poverty, and anti-Semitism, Miriam was a *balabusta*—a good friend—an accomplished cook and immaculate housekeeper. The Levines found little warmth among their gentile neighbors but were sociable people and enjoyed visiting with the few Jewish immigrants in the East End.

As friendly as they were to others, Max and Miriam were strict disciplinarians and rarely showed affection to any of their brood. With a son in his twenties and two daughters near adulthood, they were weary of raising children. Having no toys or playmates, Eddie created his own entertainment. Miriam viewed her young son's daily absences as a relief and had no patience when she learned of his misbehavior.

"What's on your clothes, Eddie?" she asked her five-year-old son one afternoon.

Eddie looked at the stains on his pants and shirt. Hastily stuffing the greasy paper deeper into his pocket, he stammered, "Don't know."

Miriam sniffed the telltale aroma of fried food and retrieved the poorly hidden paper holding limp bits of evidence. "Fish and chips! That's what you do with our money?" she said. "You stole from your own family!" The furious mother gave him a taste of what-for as a prelude to the main course he would get when Max returned home.

Miriam's answer to her son's misbehavior was the "Dirty Mummy," a tale Eddie heard often.

"There were two infants left on the counter at Woolworth's," Miriam said. "I wanted to take the other baby because she was beautiful, but you were crying, and I felt sorry for you, so I took you instead."

Eddie pictured a toothless hag who heartlessly gave away babies.

"The Dirty Mummy didn't want them anymore, so she took those bad babies to the store to sell them cheap." Miriam glared at her young son and promised, "You're a bad boy, Eddie. I'm going to give you back to her right now."

Eddie believed his mother. Threatened with going back to the Dirty Mummy, he did whatever it took to return to her good graces and avoid his father's punishment—even well into his teens.

One day, after Eddie had misbehaved yet again, Miriam said, "You have to do it, Max."

"Again?"

"He won't behave. I can't do anything with him," she said, pointing to her husband's waist.

Max's mild nature did not keep him from following the harsh disciplinary practices common in those days. There was no tolerance for a young boy's mischief. Max removed his belt and gave his son an emphatic what-for.

Half of Max's weekly income of four pounds went to Miriam for food, clothes, and household items. Sidney's salary and Trudy's manicure profits helped the family make ends meet. Miriam saved every coin given in change to buy extras like underwear and small luxuries such as bath salt.

But saving was a concept Eddie did not yet understand. He wanted what he wanted, and he wanted toys. He also wanted friends.

"There's no money for toys," Miriam explained every time her son begged.

But Eddie knew where to find some.

"Oy, Max," Miriam said as she searched in her purse. "There's not enough."

"Enough what?"

"You didn't give me enough for the week."

"I put it in your purse like always."

Miriam looked at her son playing with a brightly painted red truck on the floor. "Where did you get that, Eddie?"

He continued guiding the truck around furniture until his father's stern voice compelled him to answer. The pound Eddie stole had funded gifts for himself and the two willing boys who, for the moment, were his mates.

"Come with me," Max said as he yanked Eddie upright. "And bring your truck."

They left the house to the sound of Miriam loudly invoking the Dirty Mummy. After stops to gather Eddie's unhappy friends and their new toys, Max escorted the boys to the store.

"We're sorry, Mr. Hannigan," said Eddie tearfully. The culprits placed the truck, car, and horse on the counter. "I took my mom's money. We can't keep these."

With a stern look at the thief and his cohorts, the proprietor put the toys on a shelf.

"Can you give Dad the money?"

"I need it, too," Mr. Hannigan said as he reached to open the cash register, "but not if you stole it."

The boys left the store with heads down, each dreading their return home. Max lectured as they walked. "It's wrong to steal, Eddie. When you're caught, never run away. Even if you're guilty and want to escape, you have to do what's right."

Returning home, Eddie's father completed the lesson by administering World War III on his son's backside.

As before, the fair-weather friends rarely played with the Jew who couldn't buy them toys.

FOUR

Though hardship continued for several years following the 1945 armistice, men returning to civilian life needed haircuts, shaves, and manicures. Max and Trudy kept busy, and the Levine family income increased. By 1947, they were able to move. To the Levines, it was a better, larger home.

Though it was an upgrade, it was still woefully small.

Despite their improved financial comfort, the Levines couldn't afford to leave the East End to areas where more co-religionists settled. Again, Eddie was the only Jewish boy his age in the neighborhood, and what's more, he was fat. However, sometimes the kids allowed him to play with them.

One normal, dreary September morning, Miriam walked her youngest to an imposing building for his first day of school. Eddie was six years old. The exterior of Enfield Manor Secondary Modern School for Boys resembled a turreted castle, its beauty belying the dull gray interior.

After surreptitiously kissing his mother good-bye, Eddie looked around to see neighborhood boys scattered throughout the classroom. They were not his friends. They were Irish and English, Protestant and Catholic, separated according to their heredity and religion, all joined in poverty. The diverse groups relegated to the East End defended their territories, sought to annihilate their enemies, and unmercifully bullied anyone weaker or potentially more successful than themselves. Eddie was, in fact, the only Jew in the entire school, and thus a target for everyone, including the adults.

After only a few weeks, the class master roughly pulled Eddie's arm and said, "Come with me, Jew." They walked down a flight of stairs to the school's basement. The mystified boy noticed the pipes and wires overhead and loosely attached to the dingy brick walls. They entered a room, and the Master shoved Eddie toward a group of boys sitting on the floor. There were no desks.

Eddie remained standing and looked questioningly around the room. The silent group regarded him with interest.

"This is where you belong," the teacher said to the bewildered student and left him. Eddie looked at his new classmates and saw a strange boy with a faraway stare and another who wore a brace on his leg.

"What is this place?" Eddie asked as he sat in a space between two boys.

"We're dummies," one said.

"Stupid," another explained.

"I'm not," Eddie said.

"Hafta be. Wouldn' be here if you ain't."

"Don't know much reading yet," Eddie said. "But I'm not stupid."

Without formal testing, those deemed unable to follow the established curriculum, or who were simply different, were separated and branded as stupid. They were known as the dummy class. Their masters spent little time or effort teaching. They were simply overseers.

"The letters don' fit," Eddie told the master as he looked at the jumbled words that made no sense. "They ain't right."

23

Numbers seemed to dance on the page, changing positions, undecipherable.

The teacher had no idea what the boy was describing, nor did he care. No need to bother with the kids who couldn't learn anything anyway.

Eddie didn't bother, either. Why waste time where you're not wanted when there's so much to do outside? He repeatedly skipped school with no punishment or notice. When he did attend, his misbehavior and clowning earned him some acceptance among his classmates. Eddie's parents only knew that he went to school each day, but they had no interest in what he was doing or if he was learning. As immigrants from Russia and Poland, they had had little formal instruction and expected that, like his siblings, this son would learn a trade rather than earn a higher degree.

Eddie's clowning irritated the master and undermined his authority. The boy's Jewishness and increasing obesity made him even more unappealing. Every child was due a basic education, however, and the masters were required to accomplish the thankless task. They took their jobs as educators seriously. Caning was the established cure for all lapses and infractions, genuine or imagined.

"Go to the headmaster, Eddie," his master regularly said. "Your behavior is disturbing me."

He trudged across the playground, carefully staying on the boys' side of the painted yellow line to avoid suspension for crossing into the forbidden girls' area. He resolutely entered the administration building, walked through the gray hallway to a special narrow staircase, and slowly ascended the turret to the headmaster's office. Eddie knew what awaited. He'd been there often.

Eddie strained to open the heavy arched Gothic door and

waited until the old lady at the desk looked up. "Oh, it's you again. You know where the key is," she said as she indicated the glass-fronted case. "Pick out the one you want."

After unlocking the door and perusing the progressively thicker hickory sticks, Eddie took his choice back to the basement classroom and did as he was told. "Bend over, Jew." And the caning began. The boy tried his hardest to keep from crying, even though he knew the master would stop striking when given the satisfaction of his tears. It was a matter of pride for both. Eddie's stubbornness often resulted in wounds that bled. He thought that a good day was when, for a change, the master hit his hands instead of his behind.

Daily devotions offered salvation to every student but Eddie Levine. "In there, Jew. It's time for prayers." Each morning, the master grabbed the child's neck in a tight hold and locked him in a dark closet for the duration, exempting him from mandatory Christian observance but traumatizing him in a daily hell. He was not only singled out and punished for being a Jew, but Eddie was also required to work in the darkness, inflating soccer balls.

He was the neighborhood's sole target and regularly suffered ambushes and beatings by the Jew-hating boys. Though he was more acceptable to his dummy classmates than he had been in the general population, even the misfits looked down on the Jew in their midst. Eddie had to learn to stand up for himself.

FIVE

Miriam and Max required their four children to be home Friday evening for the Sabbath meal.

"Do I have to?" Eddie asked one afternoon. "I don't want to bathe today."

"Our people died for this," his father said. "Here, we are free to observe our faith."

Eddie sulked. He knew about the relatives who hadn't left Russia. "But I want to stay outside. I was winning."

"There's always marbles," Max said. "It's our duty to honor the Sabbath, to keep our traditions."

Eddie fidgeted as his father again launched into the story of the Levine's exodus.

"I was younger than you, *boychick*, when they came. The Communists. Your grandparents were brave to leave."

Eddie pictured the homeland they had escaped. His father had described it many times.

Their community was a ghetto in the countryside outside Minsk, Russia, the harsh land the government had designated for the most hated segment of their population. The easiest way to control their Jews. Anti-Semitism in Eastern Europe spanned centuries. The area often changed names as political domination transitioned from Lithuania to Poland to Russia. Infrequent benevolent rulers allowed Jews to live in relative peace, and during these times, some prospered, but they often endured discrimination, persecution, and slaughter. When Communists ousted the Russian czar in 1917, anti-Semitism escalated even further.

Max continued the familiar story. "My parents heard about the Communists. They would come to our shtetl soon, even though we were so poor, to take what little we had. Our lives meant nothing to them. It was my papa's decision. We had to either leave Russia or be killed." Max tearfully asked, "Can you imagine what it was like, *boychick*, to load all you can fit into a large wooden cart and leave your home forever?"

The Levines had joined thousands of refugees to trek across Europe in search of a better life. After many difficult months, they settled in England, which they thought would offer the opportunity to live in peace. With no friends nearby nor knowledge of the customs or language, the family moved into lodgings on Cannon Street in London's East End.

Winning at marbles no longer seemed important to Eddie. Even though he usually had bruises from the bullies' random punches, at least he wasn't afraid for his life. "I'm glad Zayde decided to leave Russia," he said.

"So now you understand," Max said to his son, nudging him toward the tub. "It's your turn." And the boy prepared for the Sabbath meal as expected.

Eddie's older brother had learned to defend himself by taking up the art of fisticuffs. Returning from military service in India, twenty-two-year-old Sidney saw Eddie's bruises and concluded that his brother needed instruction.

"You're going to learn to box," Sidney vowed. He taught

his chubby, clumsy brother about strategy as well as technique.

One fateful day, the leader of the bullies accosted Eddie on the playground. "Get out, you kike," the ruffian taunted as his cohorts stood ready to fight. "Why didn't Hitler take care of the lot of you when he was at it?"

This was a comment Eddie heard often. He knew about Hitler. His mother talked about her family members from Poland who were lost in the Holocaust. Sometimes she cried. Eddie was glad Hitler was dead.

"I'm gonna knock your block off, Jew!" The brawny kid played to his audience. As usual, Eddie tried to ignore the insults and impending danger, but he knew the harassment would not end unless he heeded Sidney's advice.

"I'll fight all you blokes," he answered, "but not here where the masters can see."

The boys went behind the building to escape scrutiny, and Eddie landed the first punch. He aimed for his confident opponent and pummeled him to the ground, beating him until the others disappeared.

"Don't hit me no more," the boy gasped when he saw that his friends had abandoned him.

That day, each combatant adjusted his perception of the other. No longer a victim, Eddie jubilantly allowed the coward to limp away. With their ringleader defeated, just as Sidney had predicted, they never again bothered the victorious Eddie Levine.

His reputation spread among the neighborhood boys, freeing him from blatant confrontations. With little parental supervision, he roamed the East End, and when allowed by the boys, took part in their activities. Dexterous and determined, Eddie excelled at marbles, the neighborhood pastime. He kept his smooth round glass shooter in his pocket, ready anytime for a game.

"I'll beat ya this time, Levine."

"You couldn't even beat my grandma, and she's dead," Eddie taunted. The game was a close match, but he refused to give up. He searched his pockets.

"What ya got?" The boys used anything except money to bet, and marble-shark Eddie usually won the assortment. This time, his honor was at stake.

Eddie thought about the stash under his bed but couldn't come up with anything good enough. Until he remembered.

"Wait," he said as he ran to his house. He returned with his father's gold watch—the one Miriam's parents had given Max for an engagement gift.

Then the unthinkable happened. Eddie blamed his loss on a cracked marble, an excuse that didn't impress his father when he discovered the watch was missing. As Max applied what-for to his son's behind, Eddie's yelps blended with his mother's predictions of the Dirty Mummy's coming visit.

Again, Eddie's father escorted him to face adults, instructing, "Tell them it was a wedding gift from your grandfather. Say it's not worth much, but it means a lot to me."

"Okay, Dad." Eddie dreaded the coming scene. What if the parents refused to relinquish it? What if his opponent demanded a replacement prize?

Eddie added a few tears and sincere remorse to his script, and they returned home with the gold watch.

Though his thought processes often resulted in behavior

that ended in what-for, Eddie repeatedly tried to win his parents' love and approval. He was almost seven years old when he saw a perfect opportunity.

"Here, Mom. I got these for you." Eddie had waited until the family was gathered for dinner to celebrate his mother's birthday. He proudly handed her an untidy bunch of flowers.

"These are beautiful," she said, "but where did you get them?"

"In Mr. Douglas's patch," he answered. "He's got lots of flowers."

Miriam and Max exchanged anxious glances as they realized what their son had done. The knock on their front door stifled any further discussion.

"Is this the Levine's house?" the police officer asked.

"What's the trouble?" Max said, stalling.

"Your son," the officer said as he pointed to the flowers in Miriam's hands.

The prize gladiola plants were ruined, never again to win competitions for Mr. Douglas. Half of Max's meager salary for that week went to buy replacement seedlings.

"You stole, Eddie," his father said as he gave him what-for. "You took someone else's property, and you took our money."

"I didn't mean to," his son protested. "They was just a present for Mom."

Though it was virtually stealing, Eddie learned how to increase his wealth for something he wanted. He enjoyed turning farthings into six pence. Quarter-penny farthings could be rubbed on bricks to produce a shine, then polished further with a handkerchief just before stopping at the store on the way home from school to buy penny candies. It was a favorite pastime, which boys learned from older mates, and the ruts in the gritty red bricks of the school building were proof that it had been going on for years. The unsuspecting vendor eventually noted the fading luster and realized he had been fooled into selling six one-penny candies at one twenty-fourth the price, but he could not identify which rascals had gotten away with the scam.

Innocent fun often resulted in trouble for Eddie.

Expecting a low mark as usual, he fidgeted while standing in line at the master's table, waiting his turn to have his paper graded. Each desk was fitted with an inkwell, and a ledge held pens and spare points, the nibs. To pass the time, Eddie and his only mate Ralph tested their aim by shooting the nearest nibs into the ceiling. Their classmates were delighted.

The disruption infuriated the master, who had no love for a troublesome Jewish misfit. The man's blackened or missing teeth and long black robe emphasized his great height and dyed black hair. As this frightening colossus strode to give the boy what-for, Eddie feared that the day's caning would be especially harsh. The teacher intercepted target practice by vigorously pulling and twisting Eddie's arm. When the boy clutched his shoulder and continued screaming, the reluctant master sent Ralph to fetch the school nurse.

She came running in her starched cap and pinafore and quickly directed the teacher to call an ambulance. Though the arm wasn't broken, it required tight bandaging and a sling, and Eddie was proud to arrive home in the ambulance. School protocol did not require parents to be notified of their child's accident, and when the Levines saw the ambulance and the sling, they resignedly asked, "What did you do this time?"

To parents who came from prejudice, which led to danger and death, the discrimination their son faced was minor. But the injustice Eddie endured prompted him to leave the school premises whenever possible. He tried to hide his truancy from his parents, knowing their punishment would be worse than caning. And when they discovered he was focusing on mischief rather than learning what little he could in school, Max threatened him with a list of low-paying jobs and punctuated his threats with action.

"Do you want to be a coalman, Eddie?" he shouted as he hit the boy with a wooden hanger. "Or deliver bread for a living?"

"No, Dad," Eddie answered, bending over to receive what-for.

"Hairdressing would be a good choice for you," Eddie's father often said in calmer moments. "The prices are higher, and tips are better than I earn as a barber."

School attendance was mandated until British students turned fifteen. The masters had been correct. It truly was difficult for Eddie to learn, and they had no patience nor tools to help. When all pupils reached the age of eleven and took the required tests to later matriculate to high school, Eddie had no hope of qualifying.

So, he educated himself. He observed. He stored information in his memory for later use. His future depended on learning enough to qualify for an apprenticeship. It was up to Eddie to find a way to do that.

SIX

Bobbington Air Base remained operational for many years after the war. Like many families, the Levines thanked the young servicemen with home hospitality.

"Joan's got a fella. Trudy, too," Eddie bragged to his only mate.

"I thought they had a lot of them," Ralph said. "All those pilots sorta live at your house, don't they?"

Eddie agreed. "They like Joan and Trudy a lot, but they love Mom's cooking. Dad gives them advice. We always have guys eating with us. I think they can smell dinner all the way to Bobbington."

Max's gregarious personality made him a father figure to many of the men stationed far from the lives they had known. The antidote for bombing and killing hundreds of unknown people was to seek normalcy, and the Levine's tiny home supplied a substitute family for the foreign pilots. It helped that there were two beautiful daughters and a mother who loved to cook.

American, Canadian, Australian. Ed learned to understand the funny ways the men talked, and suspected the foreigners had to work to interpret the Levines' speech too. The parents never lost their Eastern European accents, and the children's Cockney pronunciation was even more difficult to understand.

A growing boy, Eddie was a substitute for young relatives the airmen missed.

"How ya doing, little guy?"

"Hold the hammer for me, Eddie."

"Want to ride in my sidecar?"

Though he had not yet learned to count the exact tally, the boy knew there were more guests in the house than the family could accommodate. A nocturnal call of nature meant that he had to carefully make his way to the loo, trying not to step on the fingers or heads of the men sleeping in any small space they could occupy.

Their friends repaid the hospitality by bringing gifts from the base store they called the Post Exchange, or PX. They also expanded the Levine home. Miriam and Eddie watched in amazement as truckloads of lumber were unloaded, the airmen assuring them that it was just excess supplies that would be thrown out anyway. Soon construction was complete, and the crowd spilled onto the new patio to make room for more guests.

Even though the war had ended in 1945, many items continued to be scarce in England. The Bobbington pilots shared the wealth of supplies available to them at the PX, such as cigarettes, gourmet delicacies, ladies' stockings, and household goods. The family enjoyed the treats the men brought, especially the bounty one soldier showered upon them as the relatives of Joan Levine, the girl he planned to marry.

"I brought you a couple packs of Pall Malls, Mr. Levine."

"Thanks, Larry. You always remember me."

"Here're a few sticks of peppermint gum, kiddo." Eddie ran to the bedroom to hide his windfall, saving the gift for a higher purpose.

"I didn't forget you, either, Mrs. Levine. Here's your box of Schrafft's Chocolate Cherries and Crème." It was her favorite indulgence, and Larry kept her supplied. That candy was also Eddie's best source of income.

"Such a nice gift, Larry," Miriam said. "I seem to eat them so fast these days. The last box is already empty."

At school, Eddie carried out his scheme. "A penny a lick," her son declared when he had pilfered another one and brought the carefully wrapped chocolate to the older boys at school. They eagerly lined up with their coins, their tongues ready to savor the rare treat, and the entrepreneur monitored each one to be sure he didn't lick more than a penny's worth. The Jew who had few friends nevertheless had many customers for gum and chocolate. His enterprise yielded status as well as profitability. Now Eddie was more than tolerated. He was important.

Post-war life was happy, thanks to their foreign military friends. It was an even exchange: the Levines gave them a family, provided normalcy. And Eddie could spend pleasant time away from the torment at school.

Nylon stockings were the epitome of fashion in the 1940s, a necessity for young women seeking to attract the attention of the scarce men left at home. But nylon had been relegated to parachute production, and after the war, the fashion must-have continued to be among the shortages in Britain. So, women often drew a line up their legs to make it look as though they were wearing stockings.

"I have a special gift for you, Mrs. Levine," a pilot friend occasionally announced. "We got a new supply of stockings at the PX this week."

"Girls, see what Larry brought us today!" Miriam, Trudy,

and Joan always exuberantly thanked their benefactors and then followed the procedure they had devised. Each lot of hosiery was a different color from the previous gifts, and when a nylon stocking snagged and ran, it became unusable. To make their single hoses match, the Levines boiled them together with the new freshly dyed pair, and the result was an evenly colored batch.

As a military policeman keeping order among the war-weary and homesick forces at Bobbington, Larry Rennick had access to a vehicle. He often took Joan and Eddie to the base, lifting the boy into the jeep and handcuffing his wrist to the ring used to secure prisoners so that he couldn't fall out the open sides.

At the PX, Eddie couldn't believe his eyes. Everything he dreamed of was available in this wonderland. So much food just for the taking. Toy soldiers and tanks, as many as a young boy could want. So many racks and shelves of clothing…for men, for women, for Eddie. "Up you go," Larry said on the first excursion as he lifted his charge onto the soda fountain stool. "What would you like?"

"Can I have ice cream?" Eddie asked when he saw the cone an airman was enjoying.

"How about a sundae?" Larry offered.

"But it's only Tuesday…do I have to wait till Sunday?"

With a laugh, the burly MP ordered a sundae with the works, and that was an experience Eddie would never forget. "What's wrong with the ice cream, Larry? It's brown, and some of it's pink."

"Haven't you ever seen chocolate or strawberry?"

Mystified, Eddie said, "No, ice cream is ice cream. Just white." Eddie devoured the memorable treat, later describing each flavor and topping to his incredulous mother. "Pineapple, Mom. Have you ever tasted pineapple? It's the best one of all!"

"Better than banana?" his mother asked. They laughed at her rare joke, remembering Eddie's long-ago reaction to the fruit.

Then she became serious. "The Americans live like kings," Miriam said in awe. "Here, we still have ration books."

As Larry and other air crew continually brought gifts from the PX, Eddie made up his mind. "One day I'm going to live in America," he confided to his mate.

"Aw, you're daft," Ralph said scornfully. "You'll die in the East End like me."

SEVEN

Max's winning personality made customers into friends, but in the London of the forties and fifties, excellence, respect, and friendship did not equal wealth. His salary of four pounds a week plus tips kept his family poor and getting by with only the meager necessities, but true to the patriarchal attitude of the times, he would never allow his capable wife to work. Three of the Levine brothers had prospered and left the East End, but Max and Miriam made the best of their lot. They had moved to a small house in nearby Harrow. Jew or gentile, everyone in the area was poor and knew no other way of life, nor were they willing or able to find a means of improving their income.

The Levines frugally saved coins to deposit in boxes designated for specific purposes: electricity, telephone, clothes, food. They stacked pennies until there was enough to change into bobs to pay for the previous month's utility usage. The clink of a coin falling into the metal box meant that a neighbor had used the Levine's telephone and paid to cover their time.

The devastation wreaked by World War II kept food supplies low and expensive. Rationing continued for nine years following the armistice. There was never enough to eat, especially after twenty-three-year-old Sidney returned from the war, and eleven-year-old Joan was sent home after living with the family in Scotland. The occupants increased from four to six in the small house, plus the servicemen who filled the Levine home.

The Levines, like many families, grew fruits and vegetables on the allotments of land that went with each unit. Sometimes, that made the difference between hunger and famine. Like their neighbors, the family tended their patch with loving care.

Supplied by the horses, which even in the 1940s pulled delivery wagons, Eddie made his collection rounds. "Here's the bucket, Mom. It was a good day." He showed her the manure he'd gathered from the road to help fertilize their fruit trees. He headed to the small patch to spread it, doing his part to feed the family.

"Did you find anything else today?"

"No. Not much left." The rubble of bombed buildings remained as a testament to the devastation of the area. It was dangerous to sift through the wreckage in search of useful items, but Eddie often foraged in the remains and found treasure. Pots, pans, pieces of furniture.

Eddie washed his hands after handling the manure and was rewarded with a glass of orange juice. It was a prized ration, only given to children and pregnant women. Anyone older than seven could be sent to jail if caught with the precious elixir.

British citizens slowly rebuilt their cities and way of life, determinedly resuming the pleasures that added joy to the grimness of war. Everyone learned to make the most of each family member's ration coupons they received once a year. Eddie's book, based on his age of seven, gave him two ounces of sweets a week.

Every Saturday, the boys met at the corner and walked the mile to the Embassy movie theater. "Got yours, Ralph?"

"It's right 'ere," Ralph said. Both kept their hands in their pockets, guarding the valuable ration coupons.

"Wish you had a bike, too," Ralph said as they commiserated each Saturday. "It's a long way to walk when I oughta ride."

"Sometimes Dad lets me sweep the shop, so I'm getting tips," Eddie said. "Next year, I might 'ave enough to buy one."

"I guess I'm lucky me Dad found an old bike we could afford," Ralph said. "Mom makes me save any money for my clothes."

"Mine are almost boiled away. First I 'ave to pay for new pants and shirts and knickers, and then I can save for my bike. Even Sidney doesn't 'ave enough money for proper clothes yet. He 'as to put his army pants under the mattress every night to keep 'em creased."

"It's 'ard when ya 'ave to go to work in nice clothes," Ralph commented. They delayed further discussion until the walk home.

With just enough change for the cheapest seats, they bought tickets and stood in line for the candy girl, waiting to choose the treats they had anticipated for days. Eddie spied his weekly reward nestled among the array on her tray.

"A Mars Bar, please," he said and handed her the coupon. Quickly settling in the assigned seat he occupied every Saturday, Eddie excitedly tore open the wrapping and proceeded to enjoy the creamy chocolate candy. He had developed the technique of slowly licking the confection so that it lasted the entire movie, including the cartoons.

"What do you think that says?" Eddie asked Ralph after the movie as he scrutinized a large framed poster outside the theater.

Both dummies tried to decipher the words, but neither could read well enough to understand. "I'm not sure, but the picture is Gene Autry."

An older girl answered. "They're having a contest. He's going to come to the Embassy theater in the West End."

"What kind of a contest?"

"You write a question to ask Gene Autry. If yours wins, you can meet him in person."

Motivated, the boys excitedly discussed possibilities. Eddie brought the subject up at the dinner table, and the family shared their ideas.

"How about this one," Sidney proposed. "Why were the Indians driven off of their land and put on reservations?"

"What's a reservation?" Eddie asked.

Sidney wrote the question for his brother and helped find more information. By the following Saturday, Eddie had learned all about Indians and their tragic fate. With high hopes, he dropped his paper in the box at the ticket booth. Each day he waited for the post.

"Eddie!" Miriam exclaimed one day as she waved an envelope.

"For me? I never get any mail."

She pointed to a typed line. "Look, *boychick*, isn't that your name?"

"I think so." He pointed. "But what's that word?"

"Esquire. That's what it says," his mother said as she handed Eddie the letter.

He tried to read the short page, and Miriam saw that it was a struggle. Perhaps that was the first time she realized the magnitude of her son's incompetence. He gave the sheet back to her and cheered at the unbelievable news.

"I won! I'm going to meet Gene Autry!" He ran outdoors to find Ralph, breathlessly telling everyone he passed.

The next Saturday morning at the picture club for kids, the manager revealed the two winners from the neighborhood theater. At intermission, he introduced Eddie and the girl winner on stage and asked them to read their questions to the audience. Then the children learned the exciting details of their upcoming adventure.

The momentous day arrived when Eddie would go by train to the West End's Embassy Theater to meet the famed actor. An excellent barber, Eddie's father cut and styled his son's hair for the occasion. Max often brought his barber tools home to the East End on the weekend to take care of the family. "Time to get the box," he'd say, and young Eddie would fetch the special wooden crate on legs, phone books stored inside. He sat on the stack of thick books so that he was high enough for his father.

Max used Russian Bear Oil to slick down his wealthy customers' hair, but the Levines couldn't afford it for their own haircuts. So, that special morning, Miriam waited with a bottle of milk as Max completed the boy's haircut. He scooped some cream off the top and rubbed it on his son's hair, leaving it shiny and flat. Eddie put the box back by the telephone niche in the front hall and then swept the floor. He walked outside with his chest out, nodding to the neighbors to show off his stylish look.

His mother pressed the boy's pants and shirt with extra care. They had never heard of Gene Autry, but they knew it would be a great event. Their efforts to make sure their son made a good appearance assured Eddie that, for once, they were proud of him.

The winners met at the Embassy movie house in North Harrow and were escorted up the street to the underground train station. They took the "little red train" to Baker Street and joined the other winners and their chaperones, two from each picture house. Then, the group of about twenty to thirty changed platforms to board the "Big Red Train" to the West End's theatre district.

The entourage was first treated to lunch at Lyons Corner House Restaurant and then went on to the theater where Gene Autry and his singing cowboys would perform live. The winners had front row seats for the movie matinee and excitedly anticipated their idol's appearance. Eddie has never forgotten the thrill he felt when Gene Autry rode onto the stage, then dismounted his horse Champion to welcome the contest winners. The performance transported the poor boy from the East End to the world of the Wild West, and he imagined sitting around the campfire singing mournful ballads after rounding up all those Injuns and rustlers.

After the show, the children were taken backstage to meet Gene Autry, where he would answer their winning questions. To Eddie's surprise, the star's accent was difficult to understand. It was easy enough to decipher watching the movies, but now Mr. Autry's responses didn't come with action and a story line. But Eddie didn't care about the answers at all. The thrill was being in the presence of greatness.

Autry allowed the kids to pet Champion and touch his guns and holsters. The guests enjoyed dainty sandwiches and cups of tea. When it was time to leave, the children shook every cowboy's hand before heading home.

Eddie couldn't wait to tell everyone about it!

"It was great, Ralph," he reported upon returning to his neighborhood. "I talked to him. We got to pet Champion, the Wonder Horse, and Mr. Autry even twirled his guns for us."

"He's a real cowboy, all right," Ralph said in awe.

"Yep, and he said we're real cowboys now, too!" Eddie proclaimed as he demonstrated his imaginary gun-twirling skills. Several weeks later, he was thrilled to receive two signed photographs of Gene Autry and his horse. He gave one to Sidney, since it was his question that won the contest, and devised a secure hiding place for the second photo.

"Where is it?" Joan asked her younger brother.

"You can't have it."

"I just wanna see the clothes. I'll give it back to you. Promise."

"You'll tear it up."

Her sly grin confirmed his fears. Eddie always waited until Joan was nowhere in sight to take out the photo and relive the thrill of that day.

As soldiers returned to civilian life and required barbering and manicuring, Max and Trudy returned to the high-end hotel shop. Their low but steady income, combined with Sidney's few pounds earned as a hairdresser, allowed the family more of the necessities that had so recently been luxuries.

"Dad," Eddie said one evening as soon as he walked in the door. "Mr. Peabody is selling a bike!"

"That's nice, *boychick*," his father said, surely dreading what would come next.

"It's just a pound, Dad. Do you have a pound?"

"I'm sorry, *boychick*. I wish I did."

"It's old, Dad. It's rusty, but I can clean it up. I promise I'll take good care of it."

"I know you would, but we don't have the money to spare. Not even a pound." The devastation on his son's face would have broken any father's heart.

Gifts to each other were a rarity in the family, so young Eddie was shocked when one year, his father brought home a birthday surprise.

His parents beamed as Eddie hugged his shiny brand-new bicycle and then each of them.

"How did you do it?" he asked.

"It took us seven months," his mother said.

At only eight years old, Eddie Levine realized what a sacrifice it had been for his family to put away the pennies for his benefit instead of their own. Even Joan, who was always looking for a way to cause trouble for her younger brother, had done odd jobs for the neighbors and taken turns sweeping the barbershop to contribute. But it was Max's unusually generous tips the day before Eddie's birthday that made the purchase a reality and gave the boy the means to expand his world.

EIGHT

Each morning, the boys of the dummy class were allowed fifteen minutes outdoors. It wasn't for their health; the master required a smoke.

"Say, Ralph, wanna go to the airfield?" Eddie asked.

"My dad'll kill me. Can't leave school."

"What's the difference, Ralph? We're dummies. The master don't care if we go. Why should our parents?"

"Yeah, 'at's the truth. I'll 'ave a job wit me dad and uncles when I'm twelve. I'm already ten."

Both boys knew they could not qualify for the tests for matriculation to high school at age eleven. Their lives of toil would soon begin.

"So, get your lunch and let's go," Eddie said. "We'll watch the planes today." They walked away from the group and ducked around the building, carefully peeking at the master, who was languidly enjoying his cigarette and pointedly disregarding them.

At the end of exactly fifteen minutes, the master rang the bell, and the determined truants saw his remaining charges trudge back toward the basement classroom. Little Larry and Russel Axton had watched Eddie and Ralph disappear around the corner, and they lingered outdoors longer than the others.

Eddie saw them also steal away when the master turned to lead the class indoors. Entering the building until his next opportunity to smoke, the indifferent teacher seemed not to notice that four of his dummies had gone missing.

Eddie and Ralph mounted their bikes and, without another glance, left their prison behind. They pedaled over rutted streets, dodging brick piles, concrete chunks, and broken furniture—the still lingering effects of the German bombing. Homes and jobs had been destroyed, and simple poverty had become desperation for those trying to live amid the ruins.

"Where's Bruce the Goose?" Eddie asked Ralph as they navigated the roads that chilly autumn morning. "I 'aven't seen 'im in a week."

"America," he answered. "They was livin' wit' his uncle after their house was bombed."

"Too many people in the house," Eddie said with authority. Both boys had known what that was like. Conditions in the East End were not improving, and America beckoned. Their neighborhood continued to lose entire families, who were forced to relocate from the decimated area.

"My mom says for us to go, too."

Eddie kept his bike steady while glancing at Ralph. "Don't leave," he said. "You're me only mate."

That was true, though it was obvious to Eddie that the friendship had limitations. Not even Ralph invited Eddie into his home or to his birthday parties. His Jewishness branded him, and he was lucky to have even a part-time friend.

Ralph pumped his bike faster and yelled back into the wind as Eddie's chubby legs worked hard to catch up. "Don't worry!" Riding side by side again, Ralph said, "Dad says he'll not find work anywhere but the East End. Mom talks about it every night. Dad just gives her a what-for wit' a good talking to. 'At's the end of it." Ralph laughed. "Until the next night."

The nine-year-old boys pedaled slower as they approached the great arch bisecting the three-story brick building at the Spitalfields Market entrance. The aromas of raw fish and old clothes assaulted their senses.

"It ain't crowded," Ralph said. "We can ride our bikes inside and go right through."

Eddie pointed out an opportunity. "Look, Ralph. That old lady ain't watching her stand. Let's pinch some apples."

Sure enough, just inside the vast sea of booths, two vendors were gossiping with each other, and the way was clear. At this time of the morning, there were only a few housewives picking out used clothing or dinner ingredients. The early shoppers were home again, and the later ones had not yet arrived.

"Cor." Ralph grinned in agreement, and the boys executed a perfectly synchronized move. With practiced precision, they directed their bikes toward the tower of apples artfully arranged to attract the morning crowd. In coordinated and beautiful arcs, each of the mischievous truants gracefully reached out and closed their fingers around a shiny red apple.

"Stop! Thief!" yelled Mrs. Murphy as she waddled after them. Too fat to keep up as the scamps quickly pedaled away, she shook her fists. "You owe me tuppence, you hooligans!"

Once at a safe distance, the breathless, laughing boys found a secluded spot to enjoy their prizes.

"I think these are the best apples I ever tasted," Eddie said.

"I know," Ralph agreed, wiping juice from his chin and sucking it off his fingers. "We 'ave to come back."

"I never steal from the same stand twice," Eddie said. "It's bad luck."

"Hurry, Eddie! I'm way ahead of you," Ralph taunted as he jumped on his bike. They exited the market and furiously pedaled to the air base.

Postwar activities kept the Bobbington Air Base active, making the huge complex a magnet for curious young truants. "I think that's twenty!" Eddie said, not sure what number came next. They positioned themselves outside the chain link fences and watched the base comings and goings for hours, struggling to correctly count the planes practicing touch take-offs and landings. With no adult supervision or incentive to attend school every day, they could watch the fascinating happenings at Bobbington or roam as far afield as they wished.

Neighborhood boys often climbed up suitably tall trees and pretended for hours to be pirates defending their ship. Sticks masqueraded as swords, and imaginary enemies chased the fierce swashbucklers up to the crow's nest. One such afternoon, Eddie had no idea that his father was sick that day and had gone to a doctor instead of work.

Walking home, Max didn't see his son but heard a familiar voice from above. "Is that you, *boychick*?" he asked, searching the leafy limbs for a glimpse of Eddie and his friend, who ought to have been in school.

Always respectful to his stern father, the rascal-in-training answered from a high branch in a poorly disguised voice, "No, Dad, it's not me."

His father took both truants to the headmaster, who was amused at the story but nevertheless gave the boys a sound caning. When Ralph and Eddie dejectedly trod into their homes hours later, they each suffered a beating once again.

Avoiding discovery became easier with years of experience, though. The advice his former policeman father had given him served Eddie well. "Never run away if you're caught...especially if you're not in the wrong. The guilty ones always run."

Always looking to discover new abilities and refine his skills, Eddie decided one day to see how far he could take his father's axiom. The "closest to the window" game, which involved throwing rocks as close as possible to a window without breaking it, proved that it was true.

"Run," Ralph said when they saw the shattering glass fall from the second floor. It was Eddie's rock, and he stood his ground as his mates scattered in all directions.

Mr. Peabody ran out the door and shook his fist at him. "Did you break my window?" he asked breathlessly while Eddie calmly watched the man's face turn red.

Eddie looked him in the eye and then affected the most innocent expression he could achieve. Politely, sincerely, he said, "No, sir. It wasn't me. I didn't do it."

Doubtful, Mr. Peabody glared at him for a moment. "Do you know who did?"

Eddie pointed in the only direction the boys had not gone. "I saw 'em runnin' that way."

"Did you see which one threw the rock?"

"Yeah, but I didn't see his face, so I can't tell you."

The frustrated man stomped into his house to find a blanket. It would be the only covering for the hole for quite a long time. Luxuries such as glass and the craftsmen needed to install it were unobtainable even after the war.

Eddie later found his mates and relished their admiration.

He was giddy with the rush of power and excitement. It was the first time he realized he had developed a valuable skill: he could think fast and speak convincingly.

NINE

"Here's a surprise for you," Max told his son as he handed him an envelope one hot summer evening.

Eddie tore open the envelope and displayed the contents to the curious family. "We're goin' swimming!" he said. "Thank you, Mr. Glick!"

"How generous of him," Miriam said. "Your boss is a *mensche*, Max. Such a nice man."

Occasionally, the kind-hearted hotel owner gave his employees access to the pools and restaurants of the conglomerate's guests-only club, a treat he often bestowed upon his best barber, Max Levine.

"Are you ready, children? Do you have your swimsuits?" Miriam asked as she covered the sandwiches she had packed into a basket. "We'll be late for the train."

Eddie knew his parents could not have afforded to pay for such a memorable day, and he relished the experience. Never venturing into the water, Miriam watched as the family, including Joan and Larry, bobbed and swam in the pool. The couple was now wed and living in the base's married quarters.

A bevy of young women admired blond, blue-eyed brother Sidney as he flexed his toned muscles for the audience of eligible females. Army training had perfected his abilities in the water, and he included his little brother in his performance.

"You love the pool, don't you?" he asked Eddie, throwing him into the deep end. "Come on, swim to me, and we'll do it again."

Eddie kept his eyes on his brother and reached for Sidney's hand. "You're doing it!" Sidney encouraged, and threw Eddie back into the water.

Distracted, Sidney turned to the girls vying for his attention and didn't notice that Eddie was flailing, swiftly swallowing water, unable to breathe or make headway to the edge.

"Say, that kid's drowning!" a passing woman yelled, and she quickly jumped into the pool to make the rescue.

Sidney guiltily apologized to his parents and spent the rest of the afternoon making sure Eddie learned to swim.

Tired but excited about his new skill, Eddie followed Joan and Larry to their car and looked forward to staying with them in their flat for a few days. He anticipated accompanying Larry to the PX wonderland and thankfully would miss out helping his mother with the week's cleaning.

The tiny house always sparkled after Miriam's weekly regimen of sweeping the floors and carpets and polishing every wood surface. With the radio blaring for company, she and Eddie would arm themselves with cakes of wax and old cloths. Every piece of the family furniture, bought when the couple first married, gleamed after Eddie spread wax on the wood and then vigorously polished to his mother's satisfaction. On her hands and knees, she applied the same process to the floors.

It was rare that she excused her best helper from the weekly commitment, but for those few days, she needed Eddie out of her way because she had something planned. This was going to be a special gift. Without his knowledge, she had scoured the markets for ingredients to surprise her youngest for his birthday. Though farm products were slowly returning, it took two days to locate eggs and butter, which she bought at exorbitant prices. Miriam had saved for months to afford the coveted items required to bake a cake.

"Happy birthday," the family sang as everyone admired her amazing accomplishment and eagerly awaited their slices. Then, wiping crumbs from his mouth, Max took a small package from his pants pocket and handed it to the honoree.

Eddie couldn't believe his eyes when he tore off the newsprint and saw what it contained. "A watch!" He laughed with joy and jumped up to ask his mother to clasp it on his arm.

"You can thank Yanke Gelman," Dad said, smiling. "You kept mentioning you're going to be ten today, and my customers got the hint. He brought it to me last week. He told me it's been in his drawer for years, so you might as well enjoy it."

Eddie practiced walking with his arm slightly extended, the better to show off this new treasure. At school, his classmates admired the watch for the status symbol it was, but the hands moving around the face of the prized possession meant nothing to him. Eddie was an intelligent, creative, entrepreneurial ten-year-old dummy who could not tell time.

Following Larry and Joan's marriage in the early 1950s and Trudy's marriage to airplane mechanic Stan Davis soon after, the couples moved to their own homes. As the Levine's burden decreased, Max and Miriam could afford the pleasures that were increasingly available in the recovering economy.

Wednesdays were Max's short day at the elegant Strand Palace Hotel barbershop, and it was a weekly treat for Miriam and Eddie to meet him at their neighborhood movie theater. After paying for the train from work back to the East End, Max bought the movie tickets he could afford based on his tips that day. Occasionally, they could enjoy the nine-penny seats—the best in the house—but they always savored the sandwiches Miriam brought along.

The conversations on the walk home from the movies followed predictable patterns. "You know how to make a Mars Bar last," Max said.

"That's the best part of any movie," his son said.

"When you're a hairdresser, maybe you can buy two, and they'll make it through a double feature," Max responded, emphasizing his plan for Eddie's future security. The time was near for school to end for the boy. He could barely read, so his father was helping him apply for an apprenticeship.

School days had become routine. Both master and students knew what was expected, and daily prayer time became less of a trauma and more of an accepted procedure. "Levine, get out of here, we're doing prayers now," the master would prompt, and Eddie would sit in the coat room until devotions ended, no longer required to inflate soccer balls in the dark, locked closet. It was easier to endure this lesser hell until his apprenticeship.

However, Eddie soon had to endure new torture at school. The sports teacher shared his country's love of soccer and focused on turning his East End students into winning players. He placed the Jew, who was so fat he could hardly run, on defense, to block oncoming kicks and kickers. If Eddie happened to be hit or injured, it was considered by all to be no loss to the team. Eddie's parents had some idea of their son's treatment, but they knew it was futile to expose the blatant anti-Semitism. They showed little sympathy as they nursed his cuts and bruises, helping him to stoically face reality.

"There's a letter for you," Miriam said to her husband as he entered the front door after work one evening. "From Canada."

"It's from John Gillespie," he said, reading the return address. "One of the brothers. Pilots. You know, I gave them their messages when they came for haircuts at the base."

"You were the only way they had to make sure the other was safe," Miriam said, remembering. "I hope they're okay."

He perused the letter. "They say their town doesn't have a good barber."

Miriam took the page and read it for herself. "Oy, Max. They want to sponsor us to move to Ontario and open a shop. The brothers will put up the money for it."

"Why would we do that? Things are getting better here. I'm not going to Canada." He put the letter back into its envelope and stored it in a drawer, clearly intending to forget it ever existed.

That was that...for a while.

Standing on his feet as he shaved and cut hair became impossible when the ulcer that still caused Max occasional discomfort suddenly required surgery. His three weeks of recuperation dwindled the family income to a dangerously low level. So, Miriam took control.

To have their own shop, to earn a profit from other barbers' work, to say yes to the opportunity of a lifetime . . . she answered the letter without telling Max. Accepting the Gillespie brothers' proposal, she signed her husband's name and waited for the reply.

They suggested Max come to Ontario and work for a few months to see if he liked Canada.

"What have we got to lose?" Miriam urged, and when the

ticket arrived, the normally unadventurous father agreed to explore the possibility.

He found Brantford, Ontario, Canada, very much to his liking, and urged his wife and young son to join him. Larry and Joan had moved to Larry's hometown in the United States, giving Miriam another reason to accept.

"Ontario must be very close to New York City," she wrote to her husband without consulting a map to see that the distance was almost five hundred miles. "We would see Joan all the time."

After the decision to move to Canada, Miriam sold the house. She and Eddie moved to a flat. Joan and Larry did not have much money, so they had taken much of the family furniture to the United States, shipped by the military at no charge, leaving little for Miriam and Eddie's temporary home.

Miriam needed to get a job for six months to help pay for the passage to Canada, so her brother-in-law Benny employed her as a seamstress in one of his factories. She wasn't happy about it but worked a shift during the day with hours that accommodated the long distance she had to travel to the West End factory.

Every other Thursday afternoon, Miriam left work early and met her son to do their laundry.

"The clothes have to go in here," Eddie said as he perused the rows of machines.

"This is so difficult."

"No, it's easier, Mom. No more boiling."

They studied the buttons and dials. "Do I turn or push?" Miriam asked.

"Wait. I think we put the soap in here first."

With helpful advice from other patrons, the Levines conquered the laundromat.

While Miriam was working, Eddie's after-school responsibility was to light the gas poker in the pot-bellied kitchen stove. The ignited coal heated the house through pipes emanating from the stove. It was necessary to open a valve in each room to let steam escape, allowing the heat to warm the water for cooking and bathing.

Mother and son marked time, and soon their departure for Canada was imminent. Eddie gave the master his mother's note to inform the school of their plans. For two weeks, he enjoyed the attention of curious classmates and teachers.

"Where is Canada anyway?"

"What's it gonna be like there?"

"Are ya scared?"

"'At's a big ship. What if it sinks?"

"Good luck, Eddie," the master said on Eddie's last day. "Take this with you."

Eddie turned the pages of the small book and looked at him in surprise.

"So you can remember us."

Every classmate and master had signed their name, including the unfriendly sports teacher.

With inaccurate information and high hopes, mother and son prepared to set sail for their exciting new life.

PART TWO
ONE

CANADA

It was late April when Eddie and Miriam boarded the train to South Hampton and left London behind. They were finally on their way to join Max in Canada. The previous week, Miriam had sent their large steamer trunk ahead to the port. Taking their remaining suitcases from the rack above their train seats, mother and son walked two blocks from the railroad stop to the small wooden building at the South Hampton Port entrance.

Eddie gawked at the Cunard MV Britannic, waiting majestically at the dock, its two black-rimmed funnels standing proudly as white diesel smoke wafted skyward. Both Cunard and White Star flags waved in the breeze to welcome him aboard.

The White Star Line had built the ship to replace the HMHS Britannic, originally intended as a sister to passenger ships Olympia and Titanic. The British government instead commissioned it as a World War I hospital ship, and it sank after hitting a mine near Greece. Though the replacement ocean liner, renamed MV Britannic, had been well maintained and renovated since its 1930 maiden voyage, the Levines' 1954 crossing would be on an aging vessel close to the end of her useful life. To his eleven-and-and-a-half-year-old eyes, however, the ship was the most impressive vision Eddie had yet seen.

As he tilted his head to gaze at the sight looming high above, his mother pointed to the steady stream of polished black limousines delivering passengers to the entrance. "Look at those beautiful people, Eddie. We won't see them again until we reach New York." He did not understand her remark.

"Your passports and tickets, please," said a man as Eddie admired his starched white shirt and gold-braided epaulettes. He fidgeted as his mother produced the documents. The boy planned to explore every inch of this majestic ship, and time was wasting.

"Gangplank number three, Mrs. Levine."

They exited the building onto the dock and, in Eddie's opinion, walked much too slowly to the ramp that fed passengers into a gaping opening low in the ship's bow. The Levines carried their hand luggage to the designated gangplank, and the boy struggled to balance three of the smallest valises as they repeatedly slipped out of his grasp.

He saw a distant scene of elegantly dressed women wrapped in furs and handsome men wearing crisply tailored suits and stylish hats. Porters followed, handling their small bags as the procession ascended the midship gangplank to the highest deck. Adorned with gold braids and buttons sparkling in the sun, a smiling officer, whom Eddie assumed was the captain, greeted them at the railing.

"I'll be a toff someday," Eddie vowed. "I'm gonna sail first class, and I'll buy you a ticket, too."

Miriam smiled at his naiveté and said, "Save your dreams for later, *boychick*. Hurry along for now." Her urging did not keep him from watching the wheeled containers of food and supplies that perspiring workers pushed up a dedicated gangplank, directed by uniformed crew checking the items and marking papers on clipboards. It was a scene of controlled chaos, with Britannic personnel making sure everyone found their way to their correct entry.

As Eddie stepped off their gangplank into his great adventure, a young man with blue epaulettes directed the Levines to deck number four. Excitement propelled the boy to run as fast as his doughy body could take him down the narrow hallway to their cabin, where he then waited impatiently for his mother and the key to arrive.

"What a relief," she said when they entered the small accommodation and saw that the steamer trunk had already been delivered intact. When open, that trunk served as the closet, displaying hanging clothes in one side and drawers in the other, and took most of the floor space. Even in their crowded flat, it hadn't seemed as massive as it did in cabin 4102.

"Keep the trunk closed unless you need something," Miriam said. "We'll push it against the wall so we can open the door to the hallway."

Eddie looked around the space that would be his home for the next eight days, and his disappointment was clear. "We don't have a window," he said with dismay. "I want to see the waves and the birds."

"Dad could barely afford tickets for the lowest deck. We're under the waterline, but you can go anywhere you want on the third-class decks. You'll see all the birds and ocean you wish."

"At least I can 'ave the top bunk. That'll be fun," he said, knowing that his mother would never agree to climb that height in a ship rolling with the waves. Then he realized something was missing. "Where's the loo?"

"Go find it, *boychick*. You're tiring me with your energy."

Making his way through the swarm of arriving passengers relegated to steerage, he found doors identifying the two showers and three toilets that all one hundred passengers on their deck would share. At school, standing in line for the loo was

61

a familiar activity, but making an appointment for a shower would be new. No one Eddie knew had a shower. He wondered how to use this unfamiliar equipment.

Instead of reporting the critical information to his mother, Eddie wandered the halls and discovered the limitations of a steerage ticket. Padlocked, iron-grated gates barred the stairs leading to the upper-class decks, which prevented lower-class passengers from mingling with the well-to-do. He was happy, though, to find access to outer walkways and even deck chairs, which would allow him to enjoy the sea despite the windowless cabin. His rounds took him to the three third-class decks and to his surprise, there was a boy about his age, who was also exploring. They looked each other over.

The stranger spoke first. "You look like a fat Jew."

He was right on both counts. Eddie was ready to employ the pugilistic skills Sidney had taught him, but he tried diplomacy first. "What of it?"

"It don't matter. I'm Jonah. We can be mates on the ship."

And so they were. Together they found the third-class dining room, and a friendly steward slipped the boys lemon biscuits to munch as they discovered the nooks and crannies of their decks.

The levels above consisted of various-sized cabins, all larger than theirs, and dining rooms. There was even a theater, a pool, and a bar. This utopia was beyond their reach, and the curious boys only learned about it because throughout the voyage, the adults enviously imagined the upper-class goings-on. Their own small cabins offered only the bunk beds and a sink, with an occasional chair if the occupant pilfered one from the deck. The higher deck steerage cabins included the luxury of a porthole.

His shipboard mate Jonah was as outgoing and adventurous as Eddie, and they made friends with many of the crew, especially an East Ender named Arty, who said they reminded him of his little brothers. With his covert guidance, the boys discovered magnificent places passengers were not allowed. They gaped at the storage areas holding more food than Eddie had ever seen at Bobbington's PX. They chased each other through the tightly packed rows of old cars on their way to be melted down in United States steel foundries.

Jonah was a Scottish lad from the small seaside town of Greenock, and like Eddie, the youngest in the family. Four of his older siblings had sought prosperity in America and urged their parents to join them on their Iowa farms. Neither boy had a concept of Iowa or Canada and spent hours speculating about the new lives in store for them.

"My dad owns the best shop in Brantford," Eddie bragged. "He's a barber, my sister is a manicurist, and I'm gonna be a hairdresser."

Jonah eyed him with suspicion. "You mean you're gonna mess with women's hair?" He was silent for a moment after Eddie's nodded assent. Then he asked, "Are you a ponce? I don't like those blokes."

"Not me," Eddie said, laughing. "I don't like guys; I like money. Gonna make a lot and own my own shops. I just have to go to school for a few more years. Then I can apprentice."

Jonah didn't question Eddie's career path any further and ended the subject with a surprising remark. "My mom cuts our hair. We don't need any hairdresser."

Eddie hoped the Canadians were more stylish than the Scots. His future depended on that.

Occasionally, the voyage was rough, especially in stormy

weather. Miriam felt queasy even on calmer seas. She spent the first few days in bed, trying to sleep and eat lightly, so there was not much to leave her system when nausea overcame her. The friendly dining room crew kept Eddie supplied with tea and toast to bring her because she remained confined to their cabin. Consequently, Eddie was left with many hours to do as he pleased.

Eddie had packed paper and pens to occupy his time and looked forward to drawing the scenes and people he saw on his grand voyage. He spent hours stationed on a deck chair and enjoyed the attention of the bored passengers as they watched him create vignettes. His admirers often asked to keep the latest sketch. "Look what Eddie did," he heard as they passed around his pictures, and his shipboard fan club grew. Eddie's nurtured ego led him to briefly consider pursuing art rather than hairdressing.

With the compliance of their crew pal Arty, Jonah and Eddie explored the three steerage decks and the few mechanical and storage areas, but their territory was limited. One afternoon, however, the boys were intrigued to hear music. "Come on, Jonah, let's find it."

They discovered a gated stairway leading to the upper-class area. They stared at the padlock denying them access.

"You know we ain't supposed to go up there," Jonah said.

The boys learned that an orchestra played each afternoon, and though his mate lost interest after the first excitement of discovery, the music entranced Eddie. He revisited the spot daily and longed to join the elegant sophisticates above.

One day, the padlock securing the stairway gate was not completely closed. Glancing up and down the intersecting hallways and seeing no one, Eddie removed the lock, opened the gate, and tiptoed up four flights of stairs to blue skies above and beautiful people in the distance. He peeked around the corner to see if it was clear. He guessed he must be on the Promenade Deck. The grown-ups talked about the activities that took place there, available to the first and second-class passengers but not to them.

Thinking no one would notice him, Eddie took a tentative step into the open. A loud voice stopped him.

"Eddie!" the friendly crewman shouted. "You know you're not allowed here!" Arty grabbed him by the collar and pushed him down the stairs to the third-class deck. "You're gonna get me in trouble, kid. I only left the lock open, so I could get a hammer from the machine room. I should have known a smart bloke like you would figure a way to get yourself upstairs."

The memory remained, and in his mind, Eddie danced with beautiful ladies, drank champagne in crystal goblets, and joined his mother in savoring delicious treats served on silver trays. With only a glimpse of life as it could be, the boy returned to steerage with loftier dreams, determined to make a success of himself so that on his next voyage, he could enjoy the orchestra to his heart's content. In the meantime, Eddie stood in line for the loo, drew scenes and gave them to other bored passengers, and made up games to play with Jonah.

TWO

Arty ignored the boys as they passed him on their way to breakfast. "Must not have heard me," Eddie said to Jonah.

"The wind."

"Yeah. Blew my voice away, it did."

The steward impatiently took their breakfast orders, then informed them, "No eggs this morning. Here's toast for you. Porridge if you want it. Might find some scones." They took what was available and watched as the crew stacked chairs, turned tables upside down, and placed crockery in boxes.

"Let's go," Jonah said.

"We're in their way. But why?"

"It don't matter."

They had decided to revisit some of their hiding places and eavesdrop on grown-up conversations, but something was going on. The curious boys watched the crew bustling about securing deck chairs, piling the blankets in cabinets, and then padlocking the doors. At this time of the morning, their normal routine was to place the chairs on deck for the day's loungers, and these guys were never in a hurry.

Arty continued working, paying little attention to his observers until Eddie stood in his way and demanded to know what was happening.

"It's gonna be a big one," he said. "A storm. We'll be lucky to get through in one piece."

Only four days away from their destination, everyone already excitedly anticipated sailing into New York Harbor and catching their first glimpses of the Statue of Liberty. Though the ship had once or twice passed through rain and mild squalls, there had not been the same preparation and frantic activity. The adults also noticed the unusual commotion and were increasingly alarmed, asking the crew where they should station for safety and minimum seasickness.

Arty fielded questions while continuing his work, and the answers did little to comfort the passengers. "Stay in your cabin, hold on tight, and make sure everything that isn't bolted down is put away, so it don't break or hit you."

Miriam kept busy in their cabin stowing loose objects, but Eddie couldn't stay put. He and Jonah joined several curious passengers brave enough to stay on deck and watch the weather. Clouds gathered, and waves swelled. The sky darkened, the breeze gathered strength, and then the fury erupted. Thunder crashed as lightning lit up the darkness, and though he still couldn't decipher the time displayed on his prized watch, Eddie knew it was late afternoon. There should have been daylight, but it was as black as night.

Lacking stabilizers, the mighty MV Britannic rolled, dipped, and valiantly fought to stay on course in the equally mighty storm. Eddie pretended to be astride the bucking broncos, which had so thrilled him in those Saturday movies about the American West. This was the most exciting time in a voyage that had become boring. Jonah and Eddie held tightly to the slippery railing, reveling in the pelting rain and magnificent light show.

Arty came for them. "You're bonkers, kids," he yelled.

Of course, he was right. He escorted the boys to their cabins and made them promise to remain there. Miriam was in her lower bunk, moaning and retching, too seasick to admonish her son for his perilous behavior. The cabin was so small that Eddie was able to help her learn to reach the nearby sink on her own so that he could stay in his loft and draw, capturing scenes of Mother Nature's wrath.

Dinner was not served that night, and at breakfast the next morning, Eddie was the only passenger in the dining room. So many dishes had broken during the turbulence that for the short remainder of the voyage, the kitchen staff had to immediately wash dirty plates in order to serve everyone. Overworked infirmary staff treated injuries and motion sickness caused by the ship's violent heaving, while the crew repaired damage throughout the vessel.

Fear for their lives gave way to excitement as passengers watched the horizon for the first signs of New York.

THREE

Off course and two days behind schedule, the mighty MV Britannic and its passengers recovered from the tempest they would never forget and awaited their arrival in New York Harbor. Jonah and Eddie wagered dessert to the first to spy the Statue of Liberty.

Their excitement turned to disappointment when the captain announced that the ship would have to anchor outside the harbor until daylight. Arty explained that the harbor lighting was insufficient for tugs to escort the mammoth ship in the dark. Despite the delay, mother and son spent a memorable night.

"Bring your pillow and blanket, Eddie," she urged, "and we'll sleep in deck chairs." The air was fresh. The city's illuminated buildings contrasted with the night sky, providing a panorama beyond the boy's imagination. New York promised to be an awesome adventure, and excitement kept him from sleeping as he savored the sights and contemplated the day to come. They dozed until the first hint of sunrise, then joined swarms of travelers at the railing, eager to see the city in full daylight.

As the MV Britannic approached the busy harbor, the rising sun painted swaths of red and orange to frame the jagged skyline, and increasing daylight revealed buildings as far as the eye could see. It was the most thrilling sight of Ed Levine's life.

With her outstretched hand and symbolic torch, the Statue of Liberty extended a glorious welcome. Her bronze patina shone like the beacon it had been for decades, promising a new day and a new life. His education had been woefully inadequate, but even the dummy class had learned history, and Eddie knew about the statue and its importance. It seemed that every passenger was on deck, and unbridled excitement encouraged them to salute as the ship passed Lady Liberty. The crowd cried uncontrollably, cheering and hugging each other in unrestrained joy. The boys' wager of dessert to the first who spotted the statue was unfulfilled, as both were equally overcome. The waxing sun highlighted the goddess commanding her island, and she became even more beautiful as the light intensified. His tears flowed copiously, coupled with pure joy, and to this day, the memory evokes an emotional response in Ed.

As the ship passed the island and moved toward the docks, he marveled at the city growing closer. New York City shone awesome and pure in the morning light. People who are born in the United States can never know this experience of discovering America, or why immigrants kiss the ground when they come to the Promised Land.

In 1954 there was no such thing as Customs. Passports were stamped while on the boat, and passengers were free to leave the ship, officially accepted into the United States.

"Carry these bags, *boychick*," Miriam said. "I have to give the luggage tickets to the porter." As intelligent as she was, she was still subservient to men, as were most women in those days. Miriam had married at seventeen. She relied on her husband for income and guidance and was apprehensive about traveling without Max. As they descended the gangplank into the vast unknown of New York City, her nervousness transferred to her son as well, until Eddie spied salvation.

"Joan!" he shouted. His sister stood on the dock, screaming and waving. Eddie's brother-in-law Larry and his parents, the

Rennicks, had come that early morning to welcome the travelers. To the young boy, the sight was almost as awesome as the Statue of Liberty.

"Mom, we're over here," Joan uselessly screamed into the deafening noise of the crowd. The crowd yelled to the horde rushing down the gangplank to meet them.

Joan's letters had conveyed her homesickness living in New York with a new husband and strangers who were now family. She was only eighteen. Amid the chaos and hysteria of long-awaited reunions happening all around them, the Levines also kissed, hugged, and cried upon seeing each other.

"Are you hungry?" Larry asked Eddie as he claimed the steamer trunk.

"Cor,'" the young Cockney confirmed. "Yeah, I'm bloody 'ungry."

"Let's get something to eat before we go out to Long Island."

Eddie wondered what a long island was as he helped Larry load the luggage into the back of his father's monstrous car. Larry told the incredulous boy that it was the biggest model Desoto made. A typically small English car could fit in this car's boot, it seemed to Eddie. There was room for the entire family in that Desoto. He had never seen such a big automobile. After Larry's parents got into the front, Joan and Miriam in the back, Eddie didn't understand where he and Larry could sit. To his surprise, there were jump seats in the back, and on the ride it seemed that they were at a party on wheels.

With the car parked in a lot, the group walked to the restaurant. The buildings seemed so tall, so close, that Eddie imagined giants were looking down on him. The New York block was much longer than his East End neighborhood concept of a block, and he absorbed the strange sights and sounds as they made their way to breakfast.

"Do you like pie?" Larry asked as he pointed to a wall of glass doors covering small cubbyholes at Hornsby's. Obviously, it was a restaurant because it had many tables and chairs, but there was no waitstaff. Eddie saw only a cashier behind a register.

Larry pointed, and the boy stared at the cubbyhole contents. "You mean like apple pie or cherry pie?" he asked, seeing many choices through the glass. "Could I 'ave it for breakfast? Really 'ave it for breakfast?"

No one in the Levine's neighborhood could afford much filling for their pies, and to Eddie, Hornsby's slices looked mountainous. He chose the biggest one he could find. Lemon meringue. At home, they ate pie with a spoon, so when Larry handed him a fork, Eddie was confused. On occasion, he had seen people eat pie with a dessert fork along with a spoon, using the fork to cut, then eating with the spoon. Armed only with a fork, he didn't ask any more questions, he just attacked the huge piece with enthusiasm.

He took a long time to savor that pie. He had never tasted anything so good. Larry and his parents watched with amusement, and for some reason Eddie couldn't fathom, Larry's father talked to him as if he were much older than eleven-and-a-half.

"Have you heard of mutual funds?" he asked, and when the boy looked at him in puzzlement as he continued to enjoy the pie, Mr. Rennick explained the new concept. Though Eddie could barely read, his intelligent mind understood. Everything Eddie had experienced during his few hours in America told him that one day he would return and become an American, be successful, and maybe even ride a horse like Gene Autry. Eddie joined the millions of immigrants who had broken away from a far lesser life to come to the Promised Land, where anyone can succeed if they work hard.

Larry and Joan took them to their Long Island home, and his history-buff brother-in-law explained as much as Eddie could absorb about the area, though it was too overwhelming for him to comprehend how the country had become so prosperous. Visits to Macy's and Gimbels during their two-day stay bolstered his vow to return.

After a few days, Miriam and Eddie said good-bye and boarded the train for Toronto. Max and a friend met them in an Oldsmobile 98, even bigger than the Rennicks' Desoto. Eddie's fascination with cars began with those two classics, and to this day, he loves beautiful cars. Cars with lines on them. Cars that go fast.

Exhausted by the voyage and the excitement of reaching America, Eddie slept that night dreaming of investing in mutual funds, driving big cars, and dancing to orchestras. This world, so far from the East End, would be his someday.

But first, the boy needed to grow up.

FOUR

It was only sixty miles from the Toronto train station to their new town of Brantford, Ontario, Canada, but the contrast to the United States was evident, even to a boy his age. They drove through open land, a strange sight for a Cockney from the crowded East End. There were no skyscrapers as in New York City, only a few three- and four-story buildings. Brantford was a small municipality of 45,000 people, and it boasted two main streets that intersected the city north to south and east to west. The town hall faced a square, with three popular wagons, precursors of today's food trucks, selling paper cones of delicious fresh French fries.

By the time the Levines moved to Canada, all Eddie's sisters and his brother had married and were living on their own. Sidney remained in London, Joan and Larry lived in New York, and Trudy and Stan joined them in Brantford. After military service, Stan trained to be a pastry chef, whose greatest honor was his participation in creating Queen Elizabeth's wedding cake. In Brantford, he took the opportunity to buy a failed restaurant with the bonus of occupying the flat above.

Eddie and his parents only required a small home, so Max rented a one-bedroom flat over a Chinese restaurant. Though it was a single open space with areas designated for the kitchen, toilet nook, bedroom, and living room, it seemed a huge dwelling compared to the tiny house in the East End. And the Levines didn't mind the ubiquitous cooking aromas permeating their space from below.

In London, Max had worked in the elegant barbershops of the finest hotels, and after seeing the decidedly lower-class sights of Brantford, Eddie did not know what to expect of his father's new location. He saw it for the first time the day after their arrival. It was a little store, bigger than his father had described but only about six feet wide, with just enough space for four barber chairs facing a wall of mirrors and small hand washing sinks between the chairs.

The shop itself was a source of pride for Eddie's father, but the sign over the door was more important. It gave him status. Max Levine, Proprietor, Stylist for the Business Executive. Mayfair, London, England.

Each customer had his own shaving mug displayed for all to see. Max sold shampoo personalized with the client's name on the bottle. This marketing, modeled on British exclusivity and elegance, attracted Brantford's upper crust. Though two signs in the window advertised Vitalis and Brylcreem, Russian Bear Oil was a more fashionable treatment, equal to the quality of Max's Canadian customers. The dark-green liquid looked like car lubricant, and it was Eddie's special job to take the empty bottles to a tiny closet and fill them with tonic and cold diluted tea to give it the same color as the original. The gents paid fifty cents for a couple of shakes of the ersatz oil, and though it wasn't honest, the customers were happy. Max was content with that.

He was now a business owner, and the executives and prominent men in town who patronized the shop treated him as their equal. The brothers who had brought him to Brantford were influential and encouraged their friends to frequent the establishment. Max had so many customers that his pockets were full of money, which he delighted in showing his son. The wad usually consisted of only one-dollar bills because that was the cost of a haircut, but the family had never had such wealth.

The shop was a success. His father earned status as well as enough money to buy a car and even a new house. Life became much better for the Levines. But at eleven-and-a-half, Eddie still had to enroll in school.

Max discussed his son with his customers. "Eddie's very smart, but he's almost twelve, and I think we have to send him to school until he turns fifteen."

The private school headmaster was a customer and friend. "Give me Eddie's paperwork from England, and I'll enroll him."

In the London school, there were no such things as grades. There was no documentation.

"What grade does Eddie qualify for in England?" he asked. "My school begins with nine."

"I think they said he should be in grade ten," Max ventured.

The headmaster concluded that Max had no idea where his son belonged, so he sent them to the public-school principal, who was also a customer.

"Let's start him in a mixed class of sixth and seventh grade, appropriate for his age, and see how he does," the man wisely proposed.

He brought the new student into his office the first day of school and sat him in a chair next to his desk. "Your people always do well, Eddie. We don't have many in Brantford, but they always do well. We don't anticipate anything less from you, but you shouldn't expect the kids in your class to be your friends right away."

At Eddie's surprised expression, he added, "Don't worry. They'll get used to you and see that you're not so different."

Eddie wasn't singled out as a Jew like he had been in England, but everyone knew he was one. It was the rare boy who wanted to be his mate. That was reality in Brantford, Ontario, Canada, in 1955. Not much different from whence he had come and the many places and jobs he would experience after.

As in England, Eddie had difficulty with reading, math, and science. He excelled in visual and verbal subjects, which his logical and creative mind could comprehend or fake, such as art, pottery, and book report presentations...after listening to recorded synopses at the library.

Eddie loved history but found it too difficult to read a book. It was easy for him, however, to retain information from movies and earlier school trips to the Tower of London and other medieval sites. With tour guides relating the history, he could picture life as it was. He mentally stored the images along with the sights of castles, furnishings, mazes, and the specter of chopping blocks with their graduated axes for beheading various sized heads.

No longer relegated to a dummy class, Eddie was forced to read. His clipped Cockney accent faded as he adjusted to Canadian pronunciation. Though he still struggled, the Queen's English he was learning to speak made it easier to understand the written word.

After school, he continued to work in his father's shop, running errands for customers and collecting tips. Max's clientele was the prime source of income for Eddie. He launched his entrepreneurial career sweeping clippings from the floor and eagerly running to the neighboring restaurant to fetch coffee or a sandwich for the generous gents enjoying a shave, haircut, and manicure.

"I'll get it for ya," he said to them with a mischievous grin, "but it's gonna cost ya." He made a show of evaluating their tips, and his perfectly disappointed expression always encouraged the kindhearted men to give more.

Observing that Eddie was a quick-witted, energetic boy, a customer who worked for the local newspaper told him that he could earn much more money with a paper route. He sent his associate to see Eddie.

"Mr. Bradley told me to sign you up, kid. You start Monday. Meet me after school at the corner."

Eddie was enthusiastic until Monday afternoon arrived. "Here's how to attach the carrier to your handlebars," the supervisor said as he clipped the heavy steel basket to Eddie's shiny bicycle. "You got about 120 papers in those bundles, see. You fold them before you put them in the carrier."

This was not going to be easy, and then it got worse. "Here's the list. Be sure you leave the papers exactly where the customers want them."

Eddie's reading ability, though improving in Canada, made it difficult to decipher the names and instructions. But after a few days and a few loud remonstrances from unhappy customers, he got it right and was rewarded with tips when he collected weekly payment. The three-pound salary plus tips were almost worth the effort of trekking up the steps, around the back, or to the front porch. Eddie was not afraid of work, but making more money with less labor was more to his liking. He enlisted a schoolmate.

"Philip, let's go into business."

Skeptical but willing to listen, Philip agreed to partner in the newspaper delivery enterprise. For a pound, he picked up the papers and helped fold them. Soon he took on the job of delivering them for an additional sixpence. Eventually convinced to do all the work while Eddie collected payments and tips, his partner demanded more of the profit.

"But it's my route," Eddie the entrepreneur protested. "You

wouldn't have any money at all if it wasn't for me."

"Then I quit," the boy informed him.

"I do, too," Eddie said and returned to the barbershop where the tips yielded twice as much as the paper route.

Max let his son ask questions and banter with the customers, occasionally allowing him to lather a man for a shave or apply cologne.

"Wow! Thanks, Mr. Moreau," Eddie said as he pocketed the generous tip. The self-confident Cockney had learned to profit by wits and determination.

"You're a smart boy," the man said. "That'll help pay for your training."

"Righto." He would soon be fifteen, when to satisfy his father, he would leave school to begin his hairdressing apprenticeship. "I've got five years to learn, and then I'm gonna open me own shops."

The businessmen smiled indulgently at his naiveté. They couldn't know that Eddie Levine meant every word.

FIVE

The Levines were rich, at least compared to their former life. The family had lived like everyone else in the East End and had come from even meaner circumstances in Russia. But in Canada, for the first time, Eddie's parents had money, due not only to the successful barbershop but also lower taxes and lower cost of goods.

They moved to a larger downstairs flat when Joan and Larry left New York and joined the family in Brantford to occupy the upstairs unit. To Eddie, the building was a mansion. They lived like royalty with luxuries such as central heat instead of fireplaces. There was now a washing machine with a wringer in the kitchen. Miriam no longer needed to boil clothes or go to the laundromat, she just had to hang the clean items to dry. It was so easy that now she loved doing the laundry and appreciated leaving the room while the machine did the work.

Miriam considered herself wealthy. She could buy any food she wanted and didn't have to scrimp. When Eddie wanted ice skates and a BB gun, his parents had the money and didn't have to save for them. They had their own phone, though Ed's learning disabilities made it difficult to dial the correct numbers. Since in those days there were only four digits assigned to a household, with concentration, he was able to overcome the challenge.

They didn't care that for their first flat there was no garage, since they had no car, and none of the Levines knew how to drive. That changed one day in 1956 when Max arrived home with a nineteen-forties vintage two-door Ford in terrible condition. He had unknowingly paid an exorbitant price for the used hotrod but was immensely proud to be a car owner.

"Thanks for driving me home, Ernie," Dad said to his employee. "I'm going to learn right away."

"Me, too," said Miriam, "but don't we need a license?"

"Go to Mr. Harris's auto repair shop tomorrow, and he'll stamp one for you," Ernie said. "He can give you a driving lesson, too."

In no time at all, Miriam mastered the fine art. She proudly toured the town and ran errands in the repaired vehicle, a far cry from the long walks and public transportation necessary in their former life.

Though Max earned more money in Canada than he ever had in England, it was up to Eddie to help cover the cost of his clothing and entertainment, such as movies. Always looking for income, he continued working in the barbershop after school and occasionally helped in his brother-in-law Stan's short-lived restaurant. That's where Eddie acquired the useful skill of rolling ice cream rather than scooping it. Adding flourishes to his technique while joking with the patrons exponentially increased his tips. The sight of a young boy waiting tables encouraged diners to slip him a few coins, and like his parents, for the first time, he was able to afford luxuries as well as necessities.

The school principal had correctly predicted that few boys would become his friends, so when not working, Eddie enlisted his imagination and curiosity to entertain himself. Though his mother had cautioned him to stay away from the washing machine, Eddie was fascinated by the wringer. How could it hurt? Watching Miriam feed the wet clothes through the rollers, he saw how easy it was to operate.

Compelled to experiment one lazy afternoon, he placed his finger on the roller and watched his finger feed like the clothes did, advancing until his arm was firmly caught in the vise, and the machine jammed. Eddie was still a chubby kid, luckily too padded for the wringers to consume more of his arm, but the machine held him locked and in pain. Screams brought help from his frantic mother, who called her husband at work in hopes a customer would know how to release the grip.

"Hit the top bar with a closed fist, Miriam," he said, and Eddie was freed.

Miriam and a neighbor rushed him to the hospital, where an x-ray revealed the good news that thanks to being so cushioned by fat, the arm was not broken. After that, the washing machine no longer interested him.

As the family income increased, his parents were able to fulfill Eddie's repeated requests for a BB gun. Excited to get his hands on the coveted item he thought was a toy, he immediately joined the neighborhood boys to shoot pigeons off roofs, performing a community service to reduce the unsanitary droppings. They also played at cowboys, hiding behind walls and taking aim at each other. Usually, they intentionally missed, but one fateful day, someone hit Eddie in the eye. His screams, along with the general commotion of panicking boys, brought brother-in-law Larry to sort it out.

"What the hell are you doing with these?" the former soldier asked, so angry he bent Eddie's gun in half before rushing him to the hospital in a neighbor's Cadillac.

"You're a lucky kid," the doctor said after he moved the eye aside. It felt to Eddie like it was resting on his cheek. He removed the BB from the back of the socket and successfully re-secured the orb in its place. "Now, you'll have to be an extremely patient patient."

Six weeks in the hospital with eyes bandaged and sandbags to keep the boy's head immobile saved Eddie's sight.

"Can ya see now?" a classmate asked when Eddie returned to school.

"Sure," Eddie answered with a grin. "Say, I saw some pigeons. Want to get your gun?"

Sweeping the barbershop floor, running errands, and even at the age of twelve, learning to shave the gents, made him privy to adult conversations among the town executives and businessmen. They followed the latest world and local news, they debated politics and business, and they kept up with stock market fluctuations. Eddie asked questions, and one customer took him seriously.

"Take a look at this page, Eddie," he said, "and you'll understand what we're talking about. Pick a stock, and I'll explain what each column tells you about it."

The abbreviations and numbers began to make sense as Eddie carefully deciphered the information, eager to apply what he was learning.

"You can invest no more than half your savings," Max said, and his son again became an entrepreneur. His first purchase was Perrin gold, which cost less than a dime, and Eddie sold it for over a dollar. He was hooked. Like most investors, some buys paid off, and some didn't. He soon learned to appreciate the value of a dollar, and that although it is easy to make money, it is just as easy to lose it.

The young investor kept his ears open and his mouth shut,

absorbing how to run a business, how to negotiate, how to solve problems creatively. The education he gained from those men served Ed for life. Their direction gave him the tools to expand his scope past simply becoming a hairdresser to developing and building a business. Eddie dreamed about applying that knowledge. He expected to be a rich man.

SIX

Eddie wasn't alone in absorbing the lessons taught by the customers. The barbers employed by his father came from Italy and were highly skilled, but they spent their spare time analyzing stocks and investing. Their wealth enabled them to buy property. As always, Max was uncomfortable taking risks, fearful of losing his money because it was so precious. Thus, true prosperity eluded the family.

But Max Levine was an excellent barber...when he was awake. The employees brought in enough money for him to consider himself rich, so he took it easy and napped among the supply shelves in the back when he could.

Customers loved Max's gregarious personality and the shop's friendly atmosphere, and many became family friends. One owned a sporting goods store, and because he was a good customer, Max bought fishing rods from him. In his estimation, Max had progressed from barber to proprietor. He enjoyed spending his money, but without experience, he had no sense of value and paid outrageous prices. His possessions were a source of pride, however. They were tangible, usable. Evidence of his wealth.

A friendly guy, Max enjoyed camaraderie, so he signed up for a fishing outing sponsored by a local charitable organization. Unfortunately, the proprietor had neglected to sell him the proper attire. Max fished in a suit and fedora, reasoning that he was now a man of substance and should dress appropriately for his new position in society.

The sixty-mile trip from Brantford to Lake Ontario offered the local men a destination for fun and fellowship. They enjoyed ice fishing in winter and smelt fishing in the spring. Max's attire for the freezing sport made sense to him. He rejected the popular outfits in favor of his earmuffs, his long wool coat from England, and his brown lace-up leather shoes with the sensible addition of slip-on rubber overshoes. Waterproof down jackets, rubber boots, and caps with warm ear flaps did not appeal to his sense of style or economy.

His father's attire embarrassed Eddie but not enough to refuse invitations to join him on his frequent fishing excursions. Eddie went with Max and his friends when they reserved a small wooden hut standing among others on the thick ice covering Lake Ontario. One man produced an auger he had brought from home. While he drilled a hole in the ice, two others built a fire for warmth in the frigid air, and the boy helped set the fishing lines. They caught lake trout and bass until their coolers were full and drove home at twilight, anticipating a dinner fit for Poseidon. They, too, were gods of the sea.

Springtime brought the smelts and fishermen back to Lake Ontario. Eddie helped his father and his friends take large garbage cans and nets from the massive car trunks of the fifties era. As the sun rose, they dragged the water for the wriggling little fish, and in just a few hours, filled the cans with hundreds of smelts. All the wives met at the Levine home at 10:00 a.m., and as fast as the men could clean the catch, Miriam breaded and fried. Along with a steady supply of French fries, the party lasted until nighttime. She stored the leftover fish in their new freezer, and the family enjoyed the bounty for weeks.

Eddie learned more in the Canadian school than he had

in the East End dummy class. He could have continued into high school rather than dropping out at fifteen as required in England, but Max didn't understand higher education or the challenges of a teenager's social status. To him, life was all about earning a living.

"You need a profession like the rest of our family," he said. "Trying out for sports won't accomplish wealth, and you won't do well anyway. You already know the basics of my business. You can make a lot of money like your brother Sidney."

Eddie's oldest sibling was earning a fortune in London as a hairdresser, and his uncles were also successful without the benefit of an education. At fifteen years of age, having completed eighth grade to the best of his ability, the boy chose to do what he was told.

To launch his son's training, Max bought third-class ship passage and sent Eddie to London to live with Sidney and his family. He would work in his brother's elegant shop as an apprentice. His sibling had never kept a job for long and was less than mediocre as a hairdresser, but his reserved wife, Fiona, was skilled in the profession as well as in running a business. Sidney's success came from his charm and his business-savvy wife. A handsome man, who knew just what to wear to complement his wavy blond hair and tall, slim elegance, Sid's natural charisma captivated their high-end customers. He and Fiona complemented each other and built a profitable business.

Sid sent Eddie to a L'Oréal coloring school and various two- to four-week classes conducted by European hair product manufacturers. They expected that, in return, their students would believe in and promote their brands.

Satisfied after a year that he had contributed sufficiently to his brother's training, Sid sent Eddie back to Brantford, where he joined his sister Joan as a student at the Hendricks School of Hairdressing. In search of a higher income, her husband Larry had moved to Florida and worked as a bellhop in a Miami Beach hotel while attending a hairdressing school there. Joan and her toddler now lived with her parents in their Brantford flat.

"You'll love Miss Gibson," Joan said. "She studied the Harper Method in Atlanta." The Harper Method, an advanced technique of using a razor to cut hair, elevated their skills beyond any local or even European professionals. The prominent teacher also taught the 1920s flat wave, which circled the head.

"Why do we need to learn that old-fashioned style?" Eddie asked the teacher. She loftily explained that when the fad reappeared, her students would be ready and ahead of the competition. To his knowledge, it never returned.

Eddie enjoyed the class—and the female students. The prettiest classmate, the one who interested him the most, seemed to return his fascination. "You're very talented," she told him with a smile.

"And you're very beautiful," he said, hopeful that this was the beginning of a lovely connection.

They enjoyed their mutual attraction until Joan discovered that the two were spending the lunch hour in the basement getting to know each other. Still delighting in causing her little brother trouble, she told their father, adding that her brother also sneaked out of the school and listened to baseball games on her car radio. She had no idea how exciting it was to hear a no-hitter, or for a teenager to spend time in the basement for an education of a different sort.

As much as Eddie enjoyed the enlightening private lessons, he disliked the confinement of a classroom. He persisted in dodging school, just as he had in England.

Hairdressing training included the student's placement in

a shop to experience the real-life challenges of the profession. Eddie benefitted from a short after-school apprenticeship in a salon owned by two German men. He worked for free, serving as a shampoo boy, handing the stylists hair-rollers and pins, and fetching coffee and snacks for the customers. It was the hottest, most popular salon in town, and the amiable owners freely shared their knowledge. Eddie learned a lot from them.

The long-awaited day he turned sixteen—August 19, 1958—Eddie was flush with money in his pocket and ready to deal. He paid a visit to his father's customer, who owned a car dealership. Savings from years of tips in the barbershop and Stan's restaurant enabled the teen to buy a used 1949 Dodge coupe for $100 cash. No one would call it a beauty, but he had plans to bring it up to date.

"It's an easy fix," the salesman said. "Just put a board over that hole in the floor." Since the opening was at the driver's seat and revealed the street below, it proved to be a continual problem. The board shifted at every bump and swerve, but Eddie didn't mind. To him, it was a Rolls Royce.

He knew how to drive because he'd practiced on his father's car with its automatic transmission, but Eddie's new baby was a stick shift. Manually shifting gears involved coordination and constant attention. And there was the issue of a driver's license, which he did not have. With experimentation and memory of riding with friends who drove a stick, he conquered the clutch enough to make it to Red's Texaco. Max's barber customer, Red, said, "I'll take your $3.00 for a license after I see how you drive. Do you know how to park?"

"Sure, I know how to park." He didn't.

After riding for a block, Red directed Eddie back to his station. "Promise me you'll learn how to drive."

"Oh, yes, I sure will."

"Okay, give me your three dollars."

Eddie did learn, and he transformed that clinker into a hot-rod. He installed unique full disc aluminum louvre hubcaps, which he purposely put on backward so they would whistle, attracting admiring looks while he cruised the main streets.

He also installed twin mufflers, known as Hollywood pipes; took off all the chrome so he could fix and polish the dents and scratches; painted the car a sleek black; and spruced up the interior with tassels and hanging dice. Eddie's status in the teen community soared along with his self-esteem. But he soon encountered a series of problems.

First the faulty brakes failed when he and his friends were approaching a stoplight on Main Street. Luckily, most of the cars going through the intersection swerved away as the vehicle rolled through. But not all of them. The driver of the Buick ahead was his mother's friend, who, after their minor collision, was genuinely nice about getting her car fixed and didn't ask Eddie to pay. However, he had to borrow money from his father to have his brakes fixed.

The second issue was that Eddie could only afford to buy used tires for $1.00 each. He kept at least one or two spares in the huge trunk to replace the poorly made retreads because they quickly failed.

Third, the car had no back seat, but that deficit allowed the fun-loving teenager to use the adjacent trunk space and cruise the town with four guys stretched out in the back. He gained many weekend friends by squeezing four on the front bench-type seat and packing five skinny guys into the trunk area, which allowed the entire group to enter the drive-in movie and pay for only one car.

For several reasons, not least of which was that the Levines were the sole Jews in Brantford, the move to Canada diluted the orthodoxy the family had dutifully observed in England. By Eddie's early teens, the Sabbath and kosher food were no longer part of his life. His lack of observance, however, did not matter to the Christian fathers who protected their daughters from an unacceptable relationship.

"Ed's a good boy, Max, but if he doesn't stay away from my daughter, I'll take my business to your competitor." Not one of Max's good friends wanted their daughter dating a Jew, and Eddie's parents couldn't condone their son dating a gentile. Nevertheless, he had no trouble moving from one love interest to another, often forcing his father to warn him to find a new girlfriend.

Notwithstanding the few challenges, life was good for Eddie. He was learning a profession, earning tips in the barbershop, and had wheels and plenty of friends eager to ride with him. When for three weeks, his parents helped Joan and Larry settle in Florida, Eddie had the house to himself. It became the place for his friends to hang out—where no one had to clean up their mess. Where teenagers could do what they wanted without adults to disapprove.

It was a great time, and Eddie enjoyed the good life.

SEVEN

When Larry and Joan found jobs as hairdressers in Miami Beach, Max and Miriam returned to Brantford.

"You should go to Florida, too," Max said. "Learn from the stylists there."

"Your sister could use your help with their two-year-old," Miriam said, "and you can pay a little to live with them."

"They can share your car," Max added.

Now the truth was clear. They weren't making it on their own in Florida.

Why not go? So, Eddie drove his hotrod with the hole in the floor nonstop from Canada to Florida and moved in with his family, slept on their couch, and looked for work. He soon found a job apprenticing in the shop of two immigrants, who treated him kindly, and patiently helped him improve his skills. Along with the art of hairdressing, he observed their business practices and applied the wisdom gleaned from years in his father's barbershop. Combining the real-life examples that he had seen, Eddie learned what to do to be a success . . . and what not to. The student had matriculated to higher education.

Larry was still supplementing his hairdressing earnings by working as a bellboy at the Lido Hotel on the beach, and he recommended his brother-in-law to the manager. Now a fit and personable seventeen-year-old, Eddie enjoyed meeting the

well-heeled customers. His assignment was to maintain the ca-
banas and deck chairs at the pools by collecting the used tow-
els, dirty dishes, and trash. His energy and gift of gab earned
generous tips, sometimes as much as a dollar. And it was a
great opportunity to see beautiful girls in skimpy bathing suits
and to flirt when the boss wasn't looking.

"Say, you want to double date?" his coworker asked. Brandon was a bellhop in his early twenties, tan, with bleached-
blond hair, rippling muscles, and an accomplished way with
the ladies.

"I'd love to, but I can't afford it."

Brandon flashed his winning grin and said, "Don't worry
about that. The girls are paying. We're going to the races."

It was an offer only a fool would refuse. After work the
next afternoon, they changed into street clothes and waited
for their dates to drive from the Lido's front entrance and pick
them up at the employee door. A few minutes later, a convertible pulled up, and the two women flashed smiles at them. Eddie was stunned. These were not girls.

"Hi, handsome," said a woman old enough to be Brandon's
mother. "Who's your friend?"

The young man introduced Eddie to Gertrude and Mildred, nodding toward the woman in the back seat. "That one's
yours."

The foursome chatted as Brandon drove the convertible to
Hialeah. Eddie marveled as they drove under the city's imposing arch. "They sure give you a big welcome."

"You ain't seen nothin' yet," Brandon said, steering into the
flower-lined drive to the racetrack clubhouse.

"I bet the gardener is rich," Eddie said, admiring the artfully landscaped flora and its fauna. "He has to be if he works here."

"Don't you jus' love it, hon," Mildred said. "This is the most beautiful racetrack evah."

"Wow," Eddie said. "I've never seen live flamingos. There's gotta be hundreds."

"Thousands, sugah. It's an Audubon flamingo sanctuary."

Eddie had never imagined that a place like Hialeah existed. Their reservations were for the clubhouse, where the foursome sat at a table facing the finish line. After ordering dinner and drinks, they perused the race card. The ladies explained the betting process, and Eddie apologetically said, "It sounds like fun, but I don't have any money."

Gertrude and Mildred laughed as they tipped their bourbon and water glasses in a toast to the first timer. "Don't you worry," his date said, handing him a few twenties. "You just have fun."

"Good for you," Mildred said when he won a bet. "You keep it, hon." Wow! Eddie put $17.00 in his pocket, and Mildred began to look younger and prettier.

Laughing and now comfortable with each other, they returned in Gertrude's car to the Lido's employee entrance and said good-bye.

"See you soon," Brandon said to his date, and the two waved to the women as they drove away.

"Room 1509," Brandon said to Eddie.

"What?"

"That's Mildred's. She's expecting you."

Eddie got it. Payback time.

94

If Brandon had given him the full information regarding the invitation, would the young man have agreed to the evening with its terms? His limited teenage experiences with girls had seemed a natural progression, but for that one night, the teen was a gigolo. He'd received advance payment in the guise of a fun new experience, with no knowledge that there would be a price. He felt cheap, used, and guilty. But a deal was a deal, even if he hadn't been aware of it, and he had an obligation.

Brandon and Eddie parted after one more instruction. "Say, kid, if I'm late to work tomorrow, cover for me."

Eddie knocked on the door of room 1509 and found it unlocked. After he quickly paid his debt, he politely thanked his date for a lovely time. She thanked him as well, and the next day the former gigolo told the boss that Brandon had the flu.

After six months in Miami, the siblings received an excited call from their dad.

"We have a great opportunity at the Hotel Kirby in Brantford," he said. "There's space for two large stores next to each other—a barbershop and a beauty salon—and at a very affordable rent. I want all of you to come home, and we'll take both."

The Florida tourist season was over by then, and tips were drying up. It was an easy decision. Though Eddie's 1949 hotrod was barely road worthy, it was the only vehicle among them. Larry, Joan, and their young son piled into Eddie's car, and the family drove north, stopping along the way at a cheap motel. They could only afford one room and paid $4.00 for the night, the four sleeping in the one bed. The next day they drove the remaining distance to Brantford nonstop. Eddie's old car made it home, much to everyone's surprise. A month later, while Larry was driving, the engine blew out.

EIGHT

Then Eddie's life changed.

He was with his buddies at the teen hangout, Brantford's local diner, and three pretty girls approached their table. "Got room for us?"

Eddie's mates gladly made space in their booth, and they enjoyed flirting with the teenage goddesses. Petite and brunette, Carol was the quiet one. She was adorable with her perky ponytail and requisite bobby socks and loafers.

The guys left the restaurant in Eddie's hotrod. He tried to keep up as Carol sped ahead in her father's new Ford. He followed far behind but was able to take note of her route. Each day he waited for her after school, and soon they were smitten and bold enough to spend a weekend together. No one at the hotel questioned the Woolworth's wedding band they had purchased for appearances. This was true love, and they made plans for their future. Both families sought to end the romance, but the couple was tenacious in discovering ways to be together. They vowed everlasting devotion. Eddie and Carol were seventeen.

"We want to get married, Dad."

Max's reaction was predictable but not the one Eddie wanted. "Marry a gentile? Unthinkable!"

Max sent his son to England.

"Don't come back until you change your attitude about that *shikse*. And you'll have to buy your own ticket home."

Again, Eddie lived with his sister Joan and her family, who had returned to England to open a salon in London. He immediately set out to find employment to pay for the fare home to Carol.

"We've got a chair for you in our shop," Larry offered.

"No, thanks. Better to keep family separate," Eddie said.

The truth? Larry was cheap and paid minimal wages. He was a terrible hairdresser to boot. No one could learn from a guy who didn't know what he was doing. Since the Canadian hairdresser's license was not honored in England, Eddie needed to apprentice. At the Cumberland Hotel where his father had worked in the barbershop, Eddie was relieved to find that Mr. Alphonse was still the manager. He readily accepted when the man offered him a job in the beauty salon.

Mr. Alphonse was skinny and short, favoring light-colored suits, a moustache, and combed-over gray hair. He managed his salon staff strictly but fairly, making sure their wealthy clients were treated well. Eddie became one of seven apprentices who performed the menial jobs of hair washing, sweeping, and fetching drinks and snacks. Because of his experience in Canada, the renamed Mr. Ed often served as a hairdresser when the popular salon was busy.

Among the regular clients was Mrs. Goodstein of the Sandoval Sandwich Shop empire. From modest beginnings as a food supplier to caterers, three entrepreneur cousins, including her husband, had opened wholesale warehouses and hundreds of shops and restaurants throughout England.

Mrs. Goodstein was a pleasant person, and one day she brought her beautiful tall brunette daughter with her. Though apprentices were not allowed to converse with clients, Ed admired her thick hair and perfect figure. When he glanced at the stunning girl from time to time, he noticed she was looking at him too.

"Mr. Ed, would you please come here?" Mr. Alphonse said one day. Ed had seen his boss speaking with the executive manager, who oversaw both the salon and the adjoining barbershop.

"Yes, Mr. Alphonse, what can I do for you?"

"There's a request, and you're going to have to say yes."

"What is it?"

"Miss Jane Goodstein would like you to accompany her to a dinner and ball for BBC celebrities."

"You mean Simon Templar 'The Saint' might be there?"

Ed was momentarily excited at his good fortune, until reality dawned. "I don't have a tuxedo." The event was a week hence, and he was to meet her at the venue, the exclusive Mayfair Hotel.

Alphonse saw his hesitation. "Mr. Ed, I think it would be in your best interest to accept the invitation if you would like to continue your employment here."

"So, what time was that again?"

The formality of the event required Ed to rent a tuxedo and thus deplete his savings for the return voyage to Canada. He lived near his Uncle Jack and to save money had all meals with his uncle's family. At dinner, he told them his dilemma.

"Don't worry, Eddie. I'll speak with Uncle Benny, and we'll work something out."

The following week, Benny made tuxedo arrangements with his tailor, and both uncles paid for the tux, shoes, and flowers. After work on that special evening, Ed was properly attired and took the tube to the exclusive Mayfair District to await his date outside the legendary hotel.

"Hello, Ed," she said as she stepped out of the limousine in her expensive gown, casually accepting his flowers. Ed followed her into the world of his dreams. He felt like a king in the posh surroundings, though the Mayfair staff greeted Jane by name while ignoring him.

They sat at a table with distinguished people, and Ed identified Alec Guinness and other celebrities in the ballroom. When he made sure to gently bump his chair against that of the gentleman seated behind him, the man turned to face his fan.

"So sorry, Mr. Templar," Ed said as the actor gave a knowing smile.

"Actually, I'm Roger Moore," the man said and extended his hand.

Relieved at his graciousness, Ed ventured further. "We know about you in Canada, as well." What a story to tell his fellow apprentices at the shop.

Ed expected to take the tube home after the event, but Jane was insistent. "Don't worry. We'll get you back." The Rolls Royce took them to meet her friends at a restaurant owned by her family. They entered ahead of the long line of diners waiting for space in the trendy spot and were escorted to the family's special table. The conversation was about people, places, and events of which Ed had no knowledge, but the meal was fantastic.

"Should I see you home?" he asked as they left the restaurant well after midnight.

"No," Jane said, "I'll see *you* home." She paused. "Better yet, I'll let the Rolls take you, and I'll go with my girlfriend in hers."

It was an opportunity to glimpse the life of the rich. Ed went out with her again when she needed an escort, but she was way out of his league. Besides, he explained to his curious uncles, her crowd didn't know how to have fun.

With employment, Ed continued to cultivate hairdressing skills, and he soon saved enough money to buy an ocean liner ticket. Perusing newspaper advertisements daily, he found a rare deal for second-class passage to New York for only sixty-seven pounds, requiring a small deposit, which he could afford.

He had communicated with his sweetheart Carol by mail until his sister Joan reported this to their parents. Max sent a letter telling his son not to return until he ceased writing to his true love. Ed reluctantly complied.

After several months he had saved enough to pay off the ticket and set sail. Again, he docked in New York, and this time waited for his dad's friend Bob to pick him up at the pier and drive to Brantford. Ed's first action was to call Carol and explain why he hadn't written in a while.

"Hello."

"It's Eddie Levine, Mrs. Winslow."

"She's not here," Carol's mother said and immediately disconnected.

He tried again and again.

Occasionally someone answered. "Hello."

Finally! He had been waiting to hear that sweet voice for months.

"Carol, it's Eddie…" The slam of the receiver ended the call.

Determined to see his sweetheart, he went to her home. No one came when he rang the bell or knocked on the front door. The message was clear, and it broke Ed's heart.

His friends told him the truth. "It was over when you went to England."

"But I wrote for a while. She could have waited."

"Victor Harrington took your place. Right away."

"That rich bloke?"

"You didn't have a chance. He's the kind her parents want."

"Catholic and rich. I should have known."

"You were lucky to have her for a while. Her people would never have accepted you."

"And vice versa," he admitted.

Ed never saw Carol again and never ceased wondering what might have been.

NINE

"You should call my niece," insisted the regular patron sitting in the chair next to Ed's station in Brantford's most popular salon.

His sense of humor and amiable conversation excused any fault in hairdressing skills, and Mr. Ed's following grew. He was making a better income than his father ever had, and he enjoyed the social life that youth and money allowed.

"You really should ask her out," his sister Trudy said as she applied the elegant lady's nail polish. "I've seen her."

"Thanks, but I'm really busy," he said like he always did when this conversation came up. He continued addressing his client's coiffure. Why bother with a spoiled heiress when he could have a satisfying evening with any willing girl he wanted? But they persisted.

"If I take her out one time," he said, "will you stop asking?"

That one time was the first sweet taste, and then Ed bought the entire candy store. Marsha Fine was beautiful, with the bonus that she was a rarity in Canada...a rich Jewish girl.

Their evenings on the town ended in necking in Ed's flat.

"Tonight's a record," she said, laughing.

"What did you have in mind?" he asked.

"Nothing more than usual," she quickly answered. "I mean, this is the night we can say we've danced at every club in town."

"We could do that only because your dad belongs to every club in town."

She snuggled up to him and changed the subject. "I don't want to be Daddy's girl anymore. I want to be free." Anxious to escape her parents' rules and oversight, the brunette beauty's outgoing personality suited Ed's fun-loving ways.

"Can't wait to liberate you," Ed said. "It's gonna be great."

He had landed the daughter of the successful frozen fish entrepreneur Sam Fine. They were in love, which for Ed was lust, but she agreed to marry him.

The young Levines lived in Brantford in a flat on the top floor of a brand-new apartment building. His parents, Max and Miriam, lived down the hall. Marsha often chatted on the phone with her parents while she cooked dinner, and it was no secret that the prominent Fine family did not consider hairdressing worthy of their respect. They encouraged her to make Ed change vocations.

"You were so anxious to marry him that you didn't listen to us," her mother said. "Maybe it's not too late. Daddy has an offer for the two of you."

More committed to her family than to her husband, Marsha sided with her parents with each successive reminder of the luxuries she could no longer afford. Soon Ed had no choice but to agree to her father's deal. The couple relocated to the nearby town of Windsor and moved into the attic of her parents' home. For one room and a tiny bathroom, they paid rent to the Fines. In return, Ed began employment in the family business, with his father-in-law's promise that he would eventually earn a partnership in the enterprise. Thus, Ed could support their daughter in the manner she deserved.

"Not such a bad bargain," Max said to his son. "A partnership in a successful business, a beautiful wife, respect and security...not so bad."

It was Ed's job to process the daily catch of fish, removing bones and worms before the filets were packaged and frozen. It wasn't the partnership track he expected, but he didn't have to make conversation with boring customers in the salon, and his wife was happy. Though his salary was less than he had made as a hairdresser, they were able to save for a down payment on a new house.

"Here's a little something to help," the elder Fine said and generously gave the couple the money they had paid for rent. Marsha and Ed happily moved into their own home and soon were expecting their first child.

One of the brothers who had sponsored the Levines' move to Canada owned a string of racehorses and wanted to bring a few of them to the Windsor track for the season. Since he lived in Brantford and couldn't conveniently oversee their maintenance, he asked if Ed would be named as an owner. The rules required an owner to have a stake in at least one horse, and he offered Ed a free partnership in Prize Valley. All the new partner had to do was act as the go-to guy in Windsor. For this, Ed enjoyed all the benefits due to management, including special parking as well as preferred seating in the clubhouse. Marsha and Ed loved being part of the horsey set, and it was a wonderful time in their marriage.

Prize Valley never won a race until the last of the season, a claiming exhibition at which interested buyers bid on the horses. Prize Valley miraculously won its first race that day, making the Levines winners when Ed's two-dollar daily double bet gained a whopping $645.00 payout. Prize Valley was sold to the highest bidder, who took him to Buffalo, New York, where the rejuvenated nag won most of its races.

Driving away from work one day several years after the move to Windsor, Ed saw his father-in-law outside the Fine Frozen Fishery property, waving at him to stop.

"What are you doing on the side of the road, Pop?" Ed asked. "Get in."

Joseph Fine sat on the passenger side, close to the door, and didn't look at his son-in-law. "We've sold the business, Ed. Today was your last day."

Ed didn't know what to say. "My last day?"

His father-in-law remained silent as he looked out the window and then reached for the door handle.

"Don't you need me to help close it down?"

"No, it's over." Joseph Fine exited the car, never telling his daughter that her husband had offered to help. She believed his version that Ed walked out on him when he heard the news of the sale. The senior Fines retired to enjoy their wealth, though Marsha's father invested in his sons' unsuccessful business ventures and, over time, lost it all.

The couple moved back to Brantford, rented a townhouse, and Ed returned to hairdressing. He bought a salon and used the business knowledge he'd gained from years of watching and listening. It was such a success that he hired a manager and opened a second. Then a third. In all, Ed owned four shops, each designed to serve a different level of clientele.

With his attention focused on building his businesses, Ed didn't notice that his family life was suffering. The marriage deteriorated to the point that Ed was surprised when friends informed him that his wife was pregnant.

When their daughter was six months old, one of the staff said, "I'm not sure what this is about, but Marsha comes here to use the phone. I'm sure she's speaking with Paul Easton."

"Why would she be calling my hair product supplier?"

"That's what I'm wondering, and sometimes she asks me to keep packages for her. I've looked. It's always lingerie."

Of course, this required investigation. Instead of attending his Tuesday afternoon card games, Ed watched his house from a distance with a friend. They saw his wife kissing Paul as the couple exited the front door. Over the course of several weeks, Ed photographed her with three different men. He had never seen the negligees she wore.

After ten years, the candy was now stale, and a once sweet relationship had soured. The divorce was nasty.

PART THREE
ONE

CAREER CHANGE

M arsha made sure the children had no time with Ed. Though the divorce decree gave him specific visitation rights, she made excuses for their unavailability every time he came to see them.

"So sorry, but little Judith is napping."

"Oh, sorry, Teddy is at soccer practice."

"Ted will be finished with his homework soon. You can wait for him in your car."

When Ed did have his son with him, as soon as the allotted time was up, Marsha came to retrieve him on the dot.

Any hope for a cordial relationship with the mother of his children vanished one day when police arrested him for kidnapping. His son's visit had come to an end, but Teddy's tears and pleas to stay had prompted Ed to call Marsha with a change of plans.

"We all have to be in court tomorrow for the custody hearing. I'll keep Teddy with me overnight, and we'll meet you there in the morning."

"Absolutely not," she said.

"Can't you hear him sobbing? He wants to stay with me. We'll see you right on time tomorrow."

The doorbell rang, and Ed was faced with his former wife accompanied by a policeman. Ed wept along with Teddy as the boy watched the reluctant officer handcuff his father. Marsha glared at Ed triumphantly as she walked the hysterical boy out the door, a clear warning that efforts to maintain relationships with his children would be futile. The sympathetic cop released Ed to a problem worse than jail: a vindictive ex-wife. Their daughter never knew Ed. Over the years, Ted seldom saw him and inevitably lost interest.

Ed's focus changed by necessity. Without family, he concentrated on business and resurrecting his destroyed personal life.

Being a divorced man-about-town became fun, made possible by a comfortable income and lack of family responsibilities. The answering service he employed to handle clients' appointment calls also managed his nightly schedule, keeping straight for the busy bon vivant as many as three dates in an evening.

He had no interest in remarrying, but once again, someone else pushed Ed to go out with a girl. Darlene, one of his top-flight hairdressers, encouraged her boss to call her boyfriend's sister, who was visiting from the United States.

"Linda's a knockout, and she's lonesome here without friends."

"Well, if she looks anything like her brother, I'm not buying."

Ed looked at Linda when she came to pick up Darlene and wondered if he had been too hasty. "She's good-looking, all right," he said the next day, picturing her long black hair and petite figure. "But her clothes are awful. I can't be seen with someone who dresses in such bad taste."

"American styles are different from ours. Give her a try."

Eventually, he agreed to take Linda out if Darlene would give him a little peace. They met for coffee, and Ed did most of the talking. He liked her. "I'd love to take you out to dinner, Linda, but I have to ask you something, if you promise you won't be offended."

She nodded.

"Would you let me buy you a new outfit?"

"I'm offended," she said, "but I'll do it."

He sent her to a friend who owned a nice dress store in Brantford and instructed him to let her pick out anything she wanted and send Ed the bill. A week later, they dined in an up-scale Toronto restaurant, and she looked fabulous in her new pantsuit. A quiet person whose vocation was research, Linda didn't converse. The hour-long drive and even longer dinner would have been a disaster if Ed hadn't entertained her with stories of life in England and tales only a hairdresser can tell. She seemed to enjoy listening to him and was comfortable enough after a time to begin speaking.

About trees. She knew all about trees and named every species they had passed. Ed didn't care about trees, but he was beginning to care about her. After dinner, he took her to his flat.

"It's just a bachelor's place," he said. "I hope you didn't ex-pect anything impressive."

She looked around and said, "No, it's not impressive."

Ed had a goal and drew upon his presentation skills. "You know, I almost wasn't here."

Linda's curious look encouraged him. "Let's have a seat on the sofa, and I'll tell you about it."

She allowed a smile to show him she wasn't fooled but sat next to him, waiting to hear his lame story.

"It was World War II. My family lived in London. The East End. Have you heard of it?"

She nodded. He settled close to Linda and introduced her to his favorite family story.

"Don't forget your gas mask," Miriam Levine said to her husband as she handed him the small box one sunny Friday in the spring of 1942.

"It's going to be busy," he said, looping the box's cord over his shoulder. "The streets will be full of shoppers preparing for the weekend. If we're lucky, the bombs will take a day off."

"I pray for that every day," Miriam said as Max walked to the door.

"I hope people will stay out of our way so we can clear more rubble from yesterday's hits. Looters will keep digging if we leave it to them. Buildings that seem stable could be weak. What if one falls on them?"

"You have to be careful, too," Miriam cautioned. "You think that policeman's uniform shields you, but don't take any chances. Thieves won't give up easily if you catch them."

The policeman smiled at his wife as he shook his truncheon. "Don't think about falling buildings or looters...I'm ready for anything."

"I hope so." She kissed him good-bye. "I'm going to market this morning," his pregnant wife added.

"I know. It's already Black Friday again." Max chuckled.

"God forbid you should miss Portobello on the day the best peddlers show up."

"Not only the second-hand clothes," Miriam chided. "The freshest fish, fruits and vegetables so ripe and beautiful, the best cuts of meat. Oy, I should have left earlier."

"Why do you do our wash on Fridays?" Max asked. "You start boiling the clothes at sunrise, but by the time you hang them, it's late for the market."

"You expect clean clothes for the Sabbath, don't you?" Miriam said indignantly.

"Such a balabusta I married," Max said with pride. "Even with the war and a baby coming, you take good care of me."

"So, don't fuss, already. I'm late."

"It's a long way to the Notting Hill area," Max said, "and housewives from every corner of London will be there. There'll be thousands of shoppers. Everyone wants the biggest bargains before Sabbath and the weekend. Are you sure you're up to it? It won't be long now before the baby."

Miriam patted her husband's cheek and ushered him out. "You're forgetting your gas mask," she said, handing it to him. "And don't worry about me." She smiled as she patted her stomach. "This baby and I are going to find all the bargains at Portobello."

Max's assignment to help clear rubble from his neighborhood was hard work. He sweat as he focused on carefully removing debris without causing landslides. Soon, the far sounds of explosions shifted his attention. "Did you hear that?" Max asked.

"It's not close to us," another civilian policeman said. "The sirens aren't going off."

"We're safe for now. Keep working," the lieutenant directed.

"Look at him," said Max as a man ran toward the workers. "He knows something."

"Did you hear?" asked the red-faced man as he passed them. "They hit Portobello!"

Everyone knew who "they" were. The Nazis had bombed London's most popular market on its busiest day of the week.

"Miriam!" Max shrieked. Were the trains running? Too frightened to find out, he began running toward Notting Hill.

"Hundreds are dead!" another incredulous passerby reported. The news spread quickly, each alarming message adding to the terror as people flocked to the scene, hoping to find their loved ones unharmed. "Those bastards knew what they were doing! Innocent people are dead."

Max ran around rubble and thronging citizens, urgently trying to reach Portobello Road. Despite the chaos, he boldly stood in front of slow-moving trucks and cars, begging for a ride. "Please, mister, are you going to Portobello? My wife..."

Max sobbed, overcome with the shared panic that sent the crowd in one body to the dreaded destination. With scores of other desperate East Enders, he joined the growing throng and walked the six miles, arriving hours later at the scene. Max stood frozen at the sight of utter destruction.

Beyond tears, he said, "I'll find you, Miriam. I'll look under every broken cart, every pile of rubble, every heap of rags. Live for me," he pleaded. "I'm coming."

But how could she have survived?

He found the general area where vendors had been pushing their carts loaded with fruits and vegetables. Because his uniform identified him as a policeman, he gained access to the worst destruction. He waded through the disarray and began examin-

ing victims where they lay, looking for pregnant bodies, sobbing again as hour after hour, his search was unsuccessful.

By nightfall, he had examined hundreds of corpses. In clothing dirty from his futile efforts, he staggered home. Exhausted and heartbroken, Max needed rest before resuming the next morning. Nevertheless, he had to give his daughter Trudy the overwhelming news. Shoulders slumped and head bowed in despair, Max opened the front door with a heavy heart at the task ahead.

"I've kept dinner warm for you," Miriam said as Trudy moved to retrieve his plate from the oven.

He froze, wide-eyed and speechless, then blinked rapidly and stared. "Are you real?" he asked in a trembling voice, fingers reaching out to touch the apparition.

Miriam guided her husband to a near chair as he swayed and continued to gape at the unbelievable presence.

"Of course. And why not?" She laughed, wiping his perspiring brow and the smudges of soot on his face. "I knew you'd be worried," she said in a serious tone. "The news about Portobello spread fast, but there was no way to let you know I was all right."

"How could you be? The bodies, the destruction... how did you survive?"

She sat beside him and took his hand as she explained. "On the way to the train, I saw Sheila. She invited me to have a cup of tea."

"Sheila's such a gossip," her husband said, laughing through his tears, "and you always have to hear the latest."

"By the time we had three cups and talked about everyone we know, it was too late for the best bargains."

He hugged his wife tightly and with a laugh said, "Coinci-

dence decides our fate these days."

"*Call it what you will, but I say one should never refuse a cup of tea.*"

"So, you're here today because of tea?" Linda said.

"Yep. Want some?"

"Not right now," she said, snuggling a little closer. As Ed wondered how he could take this togetherness further, thunder boomed. The lights went out. It was a magical kiss and the beginning of life with Linda.

TWO

It was 1973. With no reason to remain tied to Windsor and the children he rarely saw, Ed sought a different career. For him, hairdressing had reached its financial limits, emboldening him to sell his shops and explore other possibilities.

He knew a man who knew a man who worked for a large flooring distributor. Ed interviewed with their sales manager, who said he'd call back, but the company didn't interest Ed. He landed a different job as a buyer for a chain of stores, requiring him to move to Toronto. Linda found employment in Toronto as well and moved in.

Her quiet nature and intellect offered a welcome contrast to the contentious life Ed had led with Marsha. He was deeply in love with this beautiful woman.

But, after two years together she said, "I'm leaving you."

"You can't mean it. We're in love."

"Then marry me."

"I can't."

"I'm leaving."

He had to make a decision.

"Dad, Mom, we're getting married."

The reaction was exactly as he had feared. Tears. Sobbing.

Yelling. "She's not Jewish, Ed!"

"Yes, and I love her."

His father could not accept this. "If you marry her, you will be dead to me."

"You're forcing me to choose!" Ed was heartbroken.

Linda's parents objected to her marrying a Jew and were as unyielding as the Levines. Only Ed's sister Joan and her husband Larry attended the ceremony officiated by a Justice of the Peace, followed by a dinner for four to celebrate.

Though Ed was alive and well and living one hour away, Max tore his jacket to indicate a death in the family. Miriam stopped him from going to the synagogue to say the prayers for the dead, but he sat shiva at home for his son, observing the obligatory week of deep mourning.

Ed mourned as well.

"You have to eat, Ed," Linda coaxed.

"I can't," her husband said, pushing away the bowl of soup. "Nothing interests me. It's all I can do to get dressed and drive to the store."

"How can you work? Take some vacation time until you get over this."

"I'll never get over losing my father. He killed me without ever trying to know you."

"Give it time," she said as she embraced her despondent husband. "We have years to change his mind."

"Do we?" he asked. "Dad's not so young."

Linda hugged him tighter as together they faced a future without parents.

Ed worked as a buyer for three years. But when the owner sold his stores to a larger group, it was time to find a new job. Ed's sister Joan was making a fortune selling real estate in Toronto, even though she didn't know enough to write a contract. Ed always believed she, too, had trouble with reading and math, and he suspected that their mother and Sidney faced the same challenges.

When he interviewed with Joan's real estate company, the manager hired him immediately, complimenting the winning personalities of the Levine family and promising to train him in the business. Ed would begin in two weeks.

However, Ed had seen an advertisement for a different industry, and though he had the real estate job starting soon, he kept an appointment for the interview with a large corporation. This was an exciting prospect involving sales to tire and automobile manufacturers. It was a concept that the public doesn't know about, but many industries have adopted...private brands. The Harris Tire Corporation manufactured any specification the buyer ordered under the brand name owned by the buyer. Their customers spanned the industries that used tires, such as automobile and farm equipment manufacturers, and anything else with wheels.

The HTC sales manager hired Ed before the interview ended. He eagerly accepted the job, planning to attend the real estate company's weekly training meeting and inform them that he had changed his mind.

The first item on that meeting's agenda was a surprise delivered by the owner. "As most of you know, my wife is battling cancer. We've made the difficult decision to sell to our competitors. Those of you who wish to transfer to the new real estate company can visit with the sales manager. In appreciation, each of you will find a parting check in your box."

Ed took the check as a sign that selling houses was not his destiny, and in 1976, began a twenty-five-year career with the Harris Tire Corporation.

THREE

"I've never seen you so excited about work," Linda remarked.

"I've never been this excited," Ed said.

"But you don't know anything about tires."

"That's true," her husband said, laughing. "But I'm an expert when it comes to people."

"Sure, you can make your customers laugh, but why would they buy from you?"

Ed turned from the product catalogues and sales memo notebook his boss had given him to study. "First of all, my love, HTC is a leader in the tire industry, and my customers know we'll stand behind our products."

"Yes, but you don't know anything about tires," she emphasized.

"Here's the beauty of it, Linda. My customers will teach me."

"Why would they?"

"I'll ask them. What's your best seller? Why? What else do you need? How's our delivery timing? Is it soon enough? And so on."

"Sounds good, but don't they care that you're Jewish?"

Ed considered Linda's unexpected question. "Maybe. I'm betting that they care more about their business. If I service the hell over and above my competition, it wouldn't matter if I were a green alien from Mars."

"I hope you're right."

"Now, let me get back to these books." He pored over the dancing words and numbers, determined to be a success in his new career.

Ed had never realized that such a huge market for tires existed. The biggest buyers were automobile and heavy equipment manufacturers, but those accounts went to the more experienced HTC representatives. Ed launched his career selling bicycle tires.

His first accounts were Norco, located three thousand miles away in British Columbia, and CCM, closer to his Toronto home but still hours away in Weston, Ontario. These established bicycle manufacturers sold their own brand to stores, which sold to the public. The bicycles came with tires that had no separate identity. Their customers bought based on personal relationships—if the package also included the best price to meet their specifications and excellent service. It was up to Ed to fight for the business and establish relationships. So, he developed a unique path to success.

Manufacturers required suppliers to attend meetings and educate the sales force about their products. "The salesmen know more about bicycle tires than I do," Ed said to his manager.

"They don't know that yet," Gary said. "Get up there and act like you're an expert."

Since Ed's expertise had nothing to do with tires, he said, "I can teach them about selling—and make it entertaining."

"I don't care what you do," his boss said, "as long as your numbers keep increasing."

Ed's first appearance before the sales force was a little rocky, but he was skilled at appearing proficient.

"I'm your new sales rep," he told his audience. "Ed Levine. I'm a foreigner from Toronto." The British Columbia group chuckled. Then he exaggerated the accent he had worked to lose. "Really, I'm a Cockney, mates. Even owned an old bike when I was a lad in London. Kept me tires spic-and-span, I did."

He had their attention. "You guys have already heard all about rubber, tire production, and specifications, right?" They nodded, looking at each other and grimacing. "Boring stuff, ain't it?" They laughed at the accent. "The excitement is hard to find," he said, reverting to proper English, "unless you're talking about the fun of riding that bike, the freedom a kid feels on his shiny new Road Ranger. Make the kid drool over the latest model, a million times better than the hand-me-down he got from his brother."

His audience hung on his words. "Think about presenting your new introduction to the store salespeople and taking them on an imaginary ride. What does the boy who dreams of showing that bike to his friends really want?"

"Envy," one of the salesmen said loudly.

"Right, mate. Does he care about the tire specs?"

They nodded, eyes widened. "Train your customers to sell the sizzle, the dream. Parents who want to buy the cheapest model, the one on sale, won't have a chance."

From Ed, they gained motivation and tips to increase their sales, absorbing those lessons while laughing at jokes. They wanted Ed to call on their customers with them, help them improve relationships. Through his increasingly loyal friends, his sales skyrocketed.

"We're overlooking your exorbitant expenses," his boss Gary said, "because the profits are amazing, but try to hold it down a little."

"Our competitors are spending more than I am," Ed said, "and my buyers expect dinners, trips, gifts. They're used to it. What can I do?"

The answer was virtually a blank check, and he spent weeks at a time with his friends in British Columbia. This was Ed's biggest account, bringing an income he had never achieved, and he had no intention of relinquishing the business to any-one else. But the three-thousand-mile distance made it expen-sive to return home each week, and since sales meetings were usually on weekends, the trips kept him away from Linda for extended periods.

"You're never home," she complained when Ed brought his dirty clothes and exhaustion to her. "I saw more of you before we were married."

"At least you've been able to visit your parents. I wish mine would see me."

"That's the only good thing about it. I'm lonely here with-out you."

He should not have been surprised at her frustration. Ed came up with the wrong response. "Aren't you enjoying our income?"

"It's no fun by myself." As always, Linda didn't do small talk. "If you're going to be gone like this, I want to go back to the United States."

Exhausted after weeks away, Ed reacted angrily to this unexpected demand. "I'm working my ass off to give you everything you want, and you ask me to jeopardize it all! What if my boss fires me? It's pretty clear he only tolerates me because I'm his top guy."

Linda calmly responded with the points she had prepared. "You've handled anti-Semitism all your life, and HTC won't fire one of their best salesmen, so forget those excuses. I'm just telling you that your travel is affecting our marriage."

He hugged her and changed his tone. "I never thought about that. What can I do? My best customers are thousands of miles away."

"I know it could take a while to make a change, but would you at least try to find a place closer to my family?"

"That's a possibility," he said after considering the scope of the company. "I'll talk to Gary."

"Anything that keeps you home," she said.

To Ed's amazement, his manager understood the dilemma and tried to help salvage his marriage. "I did find an opening in New York," he said a month later, "but that Yankee doesn't want a Canadian. Don't ask. He heard you were too aggressive. Didn't even care that you're my top guy."

"I don't get it," Ed countered. "Isn't a salesman supposed to be aggressive?"

The lack of results tried Linda's patience. "I can't believe there are no US openings," she said. "I'm beginning to believe what you've always told me."

"You mean about Jews in HTC?"

She nodded and said, "But wouldn't somebody be smart enough to welcome such a good salesman?"

"This is nothing new for me," Ed said. "I'll keep trying."

It was another few weeks of fading hope before Jim Masterson called.

"I hear you're knocking them dead up there," the South US Auto Division manager said, "and aggressive is what I'm looking for down here."

They laughed. "So, you've talked to New York."

"Yep, and I think we should meet. See if we can work together."

Ed flew to the Chicago Tire Show for the day, and the men spent a lunch date discussing a move. He accepted the job based in Chattanooga, Tennessee, to begin as soon as a visa could be arranged.

"You need to spend the night so we can finish the paperwork for your transfer," Jim said.

"I'd be happy to stay, but I didn't bring even a toothbrush. I have a flight reservation back to Toronto this evening."

"Don't worry, just buy what you need, and put it on your expense account. We'll make it fit in your budget."

"I don't have an expense account," Ed said, "or a budget. I give Gary my receipts, and he approves them. I don't know anything about a budget."

"No problem. I'll put everything on mine."

They shook hands in parting, and the next day, Ed returned to Toronto. Meticulous and determined, Linda began researching the visa process. The Levines had a lot to learn.

FOUR

"Corporate approved your transfer," Jim had said shortly after their 1976 Chicago meeting. "So how quickly can you relocate to Chattanooga?"

Ed visualized the tall, slender, midfifties manager beaming his boyish grin as he called to give him the news.

There was nothing good to say. The visa process had presented complications, delays, and obstacles. "I've filled out every form and talked to more immigration employees than I can count," Linda complained. "It never ends."

"What's the big problem?" Ed asked. "It's a work visa. I already have a job. The government won't have to support me. I don't get it."

"One clerk gave me the only reason that makes sense," Linda said as they discussed their frustration. "It's not a job that only you can do."

"You mean I'm taking work away from a US citizen?"

"That's what they think. You're not the only person qualified to sell auto tires."

They agreed there had to be another way. "I'll find it," Linda vowed.

Success took two years. It was August 1978 when Linda and Ed drove from Toronto to Tennessee in his rusted-out '72

Ford Pinto, praying it would not burst into flames like the news had reported others had done. They were thankful when they arrived safely in Chattanooga after a long but uneventful trip.

Ed reported for work, leaving Linda to meet the movers and settle into their new home. It was an enlightening first week.

"Glad you're finally here," Jim said. "Canada's our friend. Can't understand why US red tape took years to process."

"Thanks for holding the job for me."

"You're just the kind of guy I need, but I didn't think it was gonna happen."

"We almost gave up. Would have if Linda hadn't figured out a different way to get through to the American government."

"Fill me in. How did she do it?"

"A work visa took too long, so I resigned from the company and applied as her spouse."

"Smart girl."

"That made me the husband of a citizen. Her family agreed to testify that I'm a good guy with a job waiting, so I won't be a burden on them or the state. It was another three months till the green card arrived. I used the time to learn about automobile tires."

They discussed the geography of Ed's sales territory and chatted about a plan to introduce him to the HTC employees based in Chattanooga. "I'm anxious to get started," Ed said enthusiastically.

"Let's go over a small detail first," Jim said as he leaned forward to look Ed in the eyes. His new boss's next sentence confirmed Ed's fear that he would not like the explanation.

"There's a problem with your salary."

Ed's heart sank. Now in their thirties, the couple needed to save for the future. Had he made this life-changing move only to be poor again? Linda would never forgive him.

"I didn't realize there was an issue. Is it too high?"

"It's too low. If we pay the US dollar equivalent of your Canadian salary, you'll be below the US division's bottom salary for your status."

"Do I still have a job?"

"We'll have to give you a substantial raise, but do you mind if we do it in stages?"

Did he mind? Was Jim kidding? "Sure, whatever you need."

How would he tell Linda? Maybe he would wow his beautiful wife with dinner in a restaurant she'd think they couldn't afford. He'd be a hero! He expected their life would be entirely different now.

Jim interrupted Ed's reverie. "Spend some time with HR this morning, and then we'll go over your accounts. You need to call on them right away."

As he turned to go to Human Resources, walking on air, Ed heard, "By the way, why don't you and Linda meet the missus and me at the marina this Saturday. We'll have a few drinks and take a spin on my boat."

"You have a boat?"

"Sure. You ought to buy one, too. We have several exceptional lakes around here."

"I'm sure I won't be able to afford a boat."

"Ed, don't ever forget this: it's always better to be a has-been than a never-was."

This was a concept a salesman could embrace. Later that week, Jim dropped another bombshell.

"I've been thinking about your boat, Ed, but first, you should get rid of that dangerous Pinto. What kind of car would you really like?"

"It's not what I'd like, it's what I can afford."

"But what would you like?"

Always in love with sleek, fast cars, Ed said, "I'd kill for a Buick Riviera."

The next day Jim said, "Come on, let's go."

Ed left the dealership with keys to a shiny new car, elated but afraid of the monthly payments until Jim encouraged him with sage wisdom.

"If you drive a car like this, you'll sell like this."

The Riviera was the first in a succession. If he had kept them all, the collection would have rivaled Jay Leno's. A year after Ed moved to Chattanooga, Jim invited him to lunch.

"I need to stop by the marina first," he said and soon revealed the outing's purpose. "See that boat next to mine? It's a beauty, and it's for sale at a great price. I think you should buy it."

"You're out of your frigging mind."

By the end of the week, Ed was a captain, if only in his dreams. He mustered the nerve to tell Linda. A woman of few words, she simply shook her head emphatically "no."

"Just come with me and take a look."

His petite wife was adorable with her captain's cap perched jauntily on her brunette hair. Ed settled for first mate. They learned to sail from an accomplished seventeen-year-old hunk in return for the fun of crewing a beautiful craft. The Levines loved their next two boats even more than the first.

FIVE

The move to Chattanooga sent Ed to the majors, the big leagues. He had graduated from selling bicycle tires. Adding to the information Ed had studied while waiting for a visa, his new boss Jim Masterson further educated him on the world of automobile tires.

"Your customers will tell you what they need," he said, "so all you have to do is listen and take notes."

He neglected to mention the added necessity of following up, understanding the terminology, and offering the most competitive pricing possible.

"It might take me longer than most of your guys, but I'll be one of your best salespeople."

Ed had always known he wasn't stupid, wasn't really a dummy. His learning disabilities now had a name: dyslexia. He applied the same effort he had mustered when he first began his HTC career. After much study, he was able to decipher specification and price lists, though Jim was correct in advising him to listen to his customers. Like Ed's bicycle customers, they shared their knowledge and responded to his efforts to provide great service.

Business methods in the United States proved to be different from Ed's experience in Canada. Sure, relationships were always important. The laid-back camaraderie he was accustomed to was a matter of being available, paying for dinner occasionally, bringing a gift to the top guys, and always offering the best price and service. His Canadian boss Gary had approved relatively high expenditures because the results warranted it.

In the United States market, a salesman was *expected* to spend a lot of money on his customers.

Jim made it clear after Ed was on the job for two weeks. "You're not spending enough, Ed. The Las Vegas show is coming up next month, so make dates with your customers and show them a good time."

What exactly was a good time? He booked dinner reservations, bought tickets to the hottest shows, and customers promised orders in return.

The HTC sales force arrived before the National Tire Expo opening to set up displays, go over specials, and generally prepare for the grueling three days to come. The night before thousands of buyers would keep the salespeople busy, Ed joined a group from several companies and enjoyed a raucous dinner among friendly competitors.

"It's on me, guys," Reggie said to the rowdy assembly. "And this is just the beginning."

"What's he talking about?" Ed asked an HTC associate as everyone toasted their benefactor.

"The guy's got the biggest expense account at the table," he said. "Reggie loves being the big shot. Just be glad you were invited to join his posse."

As the party broke up, and Ed stood to return to his room by way of the casino, Reggie put his arm around his new friend's shoulder, his face close. With a conspiratorial grin, he said, "Dessert's gonna show up in an hour." He winked. "She'll knock three times."

Ed's dessert was patiently waiting in Chattanooga. "No, thanks, Reggie. That's not for me."

"Don't worry," he said as if Ed hadn't spoken. "She might take longer, but she'll get there. Too many guys this year, so the girls are making the rounds."

"No, really, I don't want that dessert," Ed said to his departing back.

To be sure he conveyed the message, Ed left the lights off, didn't turn on the television, and tried to sleep without snoring. When three knocks sounded at 2:00 a.m., he didn't make a sound or open the door.

"Anyone there?" the woman whispered as she knocked again and again. Ed froze.

Soon, he heard the three-knock pattern from a distance and assumed she was keeping her next date.

The following morning, Reggie questioned him. "What happened to you? Mia said you didn't answer."

"Sorry. I was so tired; I guess I must have passed out."

"Want to try it again tonight?" he generously offered.

"No, thanks," Ed said with sincerity.

For both moral and business reasons, this type of hospitality was not a good idea, but Ed did heed his boss's advice and entertain his customers. He was in his thirties at the time, and it was fun early on. Salespeople did what they had to do to cement personal relationships and thus drive business. If a salesperson didn't spend overtime wooing his customers, he would be out of a job, and the company would hire someone else to follow that practice. Thus, at the various industry shows and most of the evenings in cities where he had to stay overnight, Ed was in bars and nightclubs where the music was so loud and the smoke so thick he later blamed that for his subsequent hearing loss and lung cancer.

As Ed's success increased, so did his assigned territory. Travel grew to include multiple locations of the accounts based in the South. He was away from home twenty-seven days most months and often missed a night's sleep due to the entertainment policy. To stay ahead of competitors as well as his associates, who hungered to take over Ed's accounts, he regularly stayed out with customers until two or three in the morning and was awake by five to prepare for the next presentation. Ed was so sleep deprived in those days that his best rest was on the long plane flights around the country.

Money flowed like water in the nineteen eighties and nineties, and no matter the industry, entrepreneurs, who started on a shoestring, learned to incorporate supplier funds to grow their companies. Manufacturers paid cash incentives to an owner or even a buyer to use their product, creating multimillionaires in the process.

Gossip was rampant, inevitably involving extreme wealth and temptation. Whether or not the stories contained even a kernel of truth, everyone enjoyed retelling and embellishing the tales. They became legend as they spread, lore that created fellowship within an industry.

They live on:

An owner, who had accrued unaccustomed wealth, purchased a twin-engine airplane and the service of a private pilot. He was apprehended bringing drugs into the country under the guise of shipping in supplies for his business. His time in jail bankrupted him.

An aging factory owner died suddenly while visiting his

mistress in the exclusive condominium he provided her across town from his estate. She called his vice president, who called another executive. They dressed him, placed the corpse in his own Rolls Royce, and drove it to an obscure street. They positioned their boss with his head on the steering wheel so that the horn would blow. A resident came to investigate the cause of the disturbance and reported that the man was found dead of a heart attack while driving.

When a foreign-born executive was served a limp salad at a Georgia country club, he abruptly departed and drove a few miles to a small golf club where its chef always made sure to serve crisp, cold salads. He bought the club for cash.

A manufacturer built a crypt on his estate, explaining that he would be buried there when the inevitable occurred. "I'm not going yet," he said to his critics, "but when I do, this will be my final resting place."

The structure was huge, big enough to hold the remains of generations to come. When the executive died suddenly at the age of sixty, his true motive was revealed. Though the tire manufacturer had built a lucrative enterprise, the additional contributions from suppliers combined with his creative accounting had necessitated concealed storage. The crypt served as a warehouse for pallets of cash. Lawsuits to untangle the complicated money trail forced the widow to sell what assets she could and substantially lower her standard of living.

Occasionally, Ed's own experiences added to the amusing chatter traveling around the industry. An important customer enjoyed the finest things wealth could provide, including custom-made silk shirts, monogrammed with his initials. During Ed's presentation at his company sales meeting in New York, the exec spilled coffee. Ed gallantly offered to replace his stained shirt.

"Thanks," he said. "I'll call the store." After the meeting, the executive took Ed to Barney's, the elegant shop where they kept a ready supply of the man's special shirts. He chose six in assorted colors, at the cost of $500.00 each.

Already committed to the evening, Ed took that company's sales force to Chez Josephine, one of the most exclusive New York City restaurants, and prayed his boss would approve the expenditure. The sales manager promised to reward him with huge orders, but Ed was frightened he would have to reimburse the company.

"If you want me to explain, I will," he said to his boss upon returning to Chattanooga.

"About what?"

"The $9,000.00 and $3,000.00 charges on my expense account."

Jim laughed. "You mean the bills for Chez Josephine and Barney's?"

Ed nodded.

"Cost of doing business, Ed. You kept their business. That's what counts."

Jim Masterson supported Ed in every way, even when his expenses did not affect sales. His most memorable event happened in Fort Lauderdale during a tire industry trade show.

"Welcome back, Mr. Levine," the hotel concierge said. "It's

been a while since we've seen you."

"I've got to grab a nap before meeting my dinner appointment at the restaurant. There wasn't anyone at the valet stand, so I just locked my car and left it."

"No problem, sir. Give me your keys, and Mario can park it when he has a chance."

After a quick shower and a few minutes of rest, Ed hurried to meet his customers in the hotel's rooftop restaurant. When he later bid them good-bye in the lobby, it occurred to him that he ought to check with the valet.

"Hi, Mario. I'm just making sure you got my key."

Mario's puzzled expression was troubling, so Ed asked, "You did park my Cadillac, right?"

"What color was it, Mr. Levine?"

"Red."

"We haven't seen a red Caddy, sir."

The concierge apologized. Since Mario never asked for it, he had forgotten about the key. They looked for the car, but it was nowhere to be found. When the three came to the same dire conclusion, Ed contacted his boss.

"I don't know what to do. My rental car vanished, probably stolen."

"Did you leave the keys in it? Leave it running?"

"No. No."

"Then don't worry about it. The company will pay whatever our insurance doesn't. Cost of doing business, Ed."

During the show the following day, he answered a page

from the attendant at the expo's information desk. The HTC receptionist in Chattanooga had forwarded the call.

"This is Herman at Damon Norris Clothiers on Las Olas Boulevard. Are you Ed Levine?"

"Yes. What is this about?"

"Two men are here using a credit card with your name on it. An HTC Visa. They're saying one of them is you. They acted very nervously. Didn't even try on the suits they're buying."

"Thanks for calling ..."

Before Ed could continue, Herman said, "My associate just told me they dumped the clothes on the floor. He saw them drive off in a hurry."

"Was it a red Cadillac?"

Ed heard him talking to someone. "Yep."

The car was never found, and Harris Tire Corporation covered the $40,000.00 loss.

Those were the days that money flowed like water. Some lucky people floated in the rising tide, others drowned.

SIX

The Levines loved Chattanooga and small-town life. They embraced healthier eating and took up running. Their next-door neighbors became their good friends. To Ed's knowledge, the Levines were the only Jews Marge and Bill Neely had ever gotten to know.

Bill worked for a national delivery company, and his route covered the outlying regions where many drivers were afraid to travel. Though by his definition he was a redneck Southerner, at sundown Bill made sure he, too, was out of the rural areas. Even in the late nineteen seventies, the Ku Klux Klan was proudly visible in that part of Tennessee, and they often blocked many country roads. Wearing white robes with hoods covering their heads, they held rifles to emphasize that they intended to collect money for safe passage. This applied to anyone on their roads, but when Ed was in their territory, he was afraid for his life. He blew the horn to warn them and drove as fast as he could through the barricades. Ed never hit anyone, and neither did they.

Linda appreciated the Neelys, especially as her husband again traveled so much. Marge was her good friend, and Bill, the little lady's protector. Their neighbor could fix anything.

Ed called him one Saturday morning. "Bill, I have a sewer break. It's the line going into the house. Afraid it's going to flood inside. Could you come over and take a look?"

Bill confirmed the diagnosis. "Yep. You sure have a problem there, boy."

Bill phoned his friends John and Mack, and the three stood together, discussing the water bubbling up through the grass. "I think it's gonna take one. Maybe two."

"Neely, you're stupid," Mack said.

"That's a four if I ever seen it," said John.

Bill scratched his ear as he contemplated. "Yep, Mack, you're probably right. Maybe a three."

John weighed in. "No, it's four for sure."

Bill turned to Ed. "Here's the deal. We'll dig up Linda's roses, but don't let the little lady worry. We'll keep the roots wet. Got to dig a trench to get to the pipe."

It didn't matter what they would charge, so Ed didn't ask.

His neighbor aimed tobacco juice at the grass and said, "Your job is to get four."

"Four what?"

"Heck, boy. Don't you know nothin'?" He translated it in terms the former Londoner and Canadian immigrant could understand. "Four cases of beer."

"Got it."

When Bill, John, and Mack put the last spade of dirt on the last replanted rosebush, both the job and the beer were finished.

The Levines hated to leave Chattanooga, but it killed a career to refuse a transfer, and at HTC, backstabbing was rampant. Everybody wanted to move up, be promoted, even when it meant taking someone else's job. If an associate could make you look bad, you'd be out, and they'd be in. It was a matter of surviving or being run over. How did Ed last twenty-five years in the world of corporate maneuvering? He was unique. No one else did what Ed did.

"We need you in California," Jim said.

"I'm booked tight, but I'll rearrange and go at the end of the month," Ed said. "Who will I be working with?"

"Yourself. You're moving there."

The West Coast market had potential, and HTC judged Ed to be their secret weapon to capture more of it. Competition in the tire business was increasingly tough, especially in the division selling to automobile manufacturers. HTC was a supplier of a commodity with specifications any other company could provide, but with Ed's skills, the company could have an edge.

Because dyslexia prevented him from easily deciphering specification sheets and catalogues or understanding written pages of suggested sales pitches, Ed was forced to create his own methods. They were successful. He had to work harder than his competitors, both in his company and in the tire industry. He had to be more innovative than others, rely on his own unique skills. At meetings, when all other associates took notes, Ed utilized methods that made sense to him. Memorization exercises. Pictures and drawings rather than words. Association of key points using symbols to trigger the information in his mind. His sales figures proved his success.

New United Motor Manufacturing, Inc. (NUMMI) was an automobile company in California, jointly owned by General Motors and Toyota, and the sales manager made an offer Linda encouraged her husband to accept: join an all-expense-paid trip for NUMMI's biggest customers. They cruised out of San Diego with three hundred car dealers aboard, and Ed presented sessions on sales training and motivation. He spent many additional hours individually consulting with NUMMI customers, who were interested in discussing his marketing ideas. Even after disembarking, small groups wanted to hear more about his training and motivational presentations. They booked him to speak to their sales forces.

Recognizing his talent, HTC encouraged Ed to develop training curricula and materials for the company. His availability as a sales trainer and motivational speaker became a valuable service that HTC offered to their customers' technical and support staff as well as their salespeople. As a result, commitments to speak at conferences and meetings kept Ed in the air and living in hotels most of each month. He won the dubious award for being on the road more than any other person in the HTC division.

One memorable day, he gave a morning speech in Fort Lauderdale, spoke at a lunch session in Dallas, and appeared for a dinner presentation in Los Angeles. Hotels in Dallas and Florida each designated a specific room for him, booked for a year, and he kept toiletries in the bathrooms and clothes in the closets. The airline and hotel points Ed accrued surely set records.

However, younger management began to replace the old guard, and with their departure, the Harris Tire Corporation culture became more narcissistic.

"Things are changing," Ed lamented to Linda. "I never had any friends at work, but now it feels like everyone's my enemy."

"What do you mean?"

"The young guys want my job. They're telling my boss I'm out of date, don't relate to the customers. That kind of thing."

"Is any of it true?"

"My sales figures say it's not."

"And what about all the awards you've won, the training programs you've developed? That's got to count."

"Ought to, but that's old news. These new guys want to build their careers. They're taking over everything I created. These days, it's every man for himself."

Sure enough, the new West Coast manager was not on the job long before he heard exaggerated complaints from jealous associates. He called Ed into his office.

"HTC wastes a lot of money on you," Colby Arnold said. "I think you can spend much less with the same result."

"You're the boss," Ed said, "but with due respect, you've never seen me in action."

Red-faced, Colby responded to the challenge. "I'm going with you tomorrow, and I'll take notes. You'll see you can streamline."

Ed had perfected his presentations to include a magician for a short opening act, and during those few minutes, Colby furiously scribbled on a pocket-sized spiral pad. The audience paid rapt attention. When Ed made his entrance, they were already in a receptive mood and expecting to continue the good time. They hung on to his every word, rewarding him with laughter and applause. Ed taught communication skills, time management, and alternative ways to present products. Colby barely looked up as he wrote page after page of notes. Then it was time for the final segment.

"It's your turn," Ed said to the room full of the sales staff of the division's biggest customer. "What do you want to know?"

A few questions asked for more details about the topics

he had presented, but most of the remarks complimented and thanked him for educating them in such a painless manner.

Ed and his young boss walked to the exit. "Give me your notes. I'll study them tonight."

Colby took the pad from his pocket, tore out the pages he had filled, and threw them in the trash can by the front door. "Forget it," he growled. "Those troublemakers don't know what they're talking about. Just keep doing what you're doing."

Ed didn't make customers; he made friends…an important concept that holds true for any business. His popularity spread. When travel expenses to send him all over the United States became too great to justify keeping him in California, Colby sent Ed to the more logistically practical Atlanta. Jim Masterson was again Ed's boss.

Throughout his HTC tenure, Ed had noticed that he was the only Jew. Before the company acknowledged his special talent for speaking, he had applied for and gotten various promotions, but each was rescinded prior to assuming the responsibility. Ed sensed that the change occurred when the prospective new boss learned his religion. Once, after a few drinks following a hard day at the Las Vegas expo, he had the courage to initiate a bold conversation with his mentor.

"Jim, you're a straight-up guy. Can I ask you a question?"

As he chugged the last of his scotch and ordered another, Jim nodded.

Ed asked, "Are there any other Jews in this company? Besides me, I mean." Ed waited for his audacity to register. When Jim cleared his throat and stirred the ice in his fresh drink, Ed knew he had posed a question his boss didn't want to answer.

"We're not having this conversation," he said in a tone so low Ed could barely hear him.

"What conversation?"

"The one where I tell you HTC needs diversity. Every company must report diversity. You're our Jew."

Of course. He had always been the lone Jew.

"But you do a helluva job, Ed. Wouldn't have kept you if you didn't."

"Thanks, Jim," he said with sincerity. "You gave me a great opportunity, and you're a wonderful boss."

Over time, Ed's innovative programs helped increase the division's business to the extent that his success, among other causes, made him and scores of others unnecessary. The company no longer needed as many personnel courting automobile manufacturers. Harris Tire Corporation could not justify the large expenses and salaries of a mature force, who had done such an excellent job that the business could do just as well without them. After twenty-five years, along with hundreds of others in the division, Ed Levine was downsized.

SEVEN

Harris Tire Company respected the law. They had to. Canada's Human Rights Act and the USA's Civil Rights Act dictated that corporations must achieve and, as his boss had revealed, also document diversity among their employees. Everyone knew Ed was the token Jew. That didn't mean they liked it.

Occasional diversity training did nothing to change the anti-Semitism lurking below the surface. Other than Jim Masterson, Ed had no real friends at work. The new regime replaced his supporters with bosses who made it clear that Ed did not fit. Suddenly racist jokes and remarks were the norm, meant for him to overhear.

This did not trouble him. His skills had served him well in his business and personal life, and racism was just a fact.

Downsizing the division was a decision that was good for the bottom line, but HTC wanted to be fair and keep their good employees. Those who wanted to remain with the company had ninety days to apply for other positions.

Ed had many good interviews with other divisions and received positive feedback, so he expected a variety of offers. It was just a matter of the managers speaking with Rick Johnson, his current boss. However, all possibilities disappeared after those discussions. Ed knew that Rick was responsible.

He had to find employment elsewhere.

He immediately secured a position with a well-known company that sold tires produced by HTC. Ed's first day would be at the national sales meeting in Dallas. He would arrive on Saturday morning and go directly to the meeting to be introduced as the new vice president of sales. There couldn't have been a better fit for him. After all, he had just spent twenty-five years selling their premier brand.

Friday night, Ed was packed, airline tickets and new business cards in hand. He was ready to start his new job, to make a difference. At 9:00 p.m., the phone rang. It was the company's president.

"Ed, it's George Anderson."

"Thanks for checking on me. I'm prepared and rarin' to get started."

George cleared his throat. There was a pause, and then, "Please don't come to the meeting."

Ed's heart raced as he tried to control his shaking voice. "Is something wrong?"

Another pause. "We can't hire you."

He stifled a gasp. "Why?"

"Just got a call from Rick Johnson."

Ed slapped his thigh to keep from expressing his anger. Better to stay professional. "My former boss was never a fan."

"He told me we couldn't go through with it. If we do, we'll lose their line."

Ed couldn't believe it. "You're telling me that asshole threatened you? He must really hate me."

"I'm so sorry, Ed. I don't know what to say. I know it's not fair to you. You'd be a great sales manager."

They both were embarrassed. No apologies could hide the ugly unspoken truth. Ed was a Jew. Jews were not welcome here. Or there. And sometimes, not anywhere. If there had been a theme to Ed's life, this was it. No matter his achievements, to the world Ed Levine was first and foremost—and unforgivably—a Jew.

"I get it," Ed said. "Good-bye, George."

Ed held the phone after George had disconnected, too stunned to lay it down. He should have suspected something like this would happen. Would his future depend on HTC references? How could he tell Linda? First, Ed needed to calm down, allow his heart rate to slow and his anger to cool.

He turned to his four-legged friend, the last of the retired racing greyhounds the Levines had rescued from euthanasia. "Come on, Ben. We're going for a walk. We have a lot to discuss."

EIGHT

It was 2001. Ed was unemployed, and his sixtieth birthday was approaching.

"We have money," he said.

"Enough to last another twenty years?" Linda asked.

"If the stock market doesn't crash," Ed said. Linda didn't laugh. "I could retire for now, and if things don't look good later, find a job."

"Who will remember you later?" she asked. "Your reputation and connections are in place right now."

Ed nodded, but he knew there was even more to it. "You just want me out of your way."

"There's that," she said. "And I like those paychecks."

"Yeah, I don't want to lower our standard of living. Speaking gigs will help, but that's not a guarantee."

"You have to find a job, Ed. I don't want to be eighty and destitute."

He was gratified to receive encouraging calls from sales managers, car dealers, random people related to the tire industry who had heard he'd been terminated. They booked him for speaking and consulting engagements, which provided enough supplemental income to satisfy Linda. The Levines were becoming accustomed to their new normal when Ed heard from Pancho Segovia, a former competitor and good friend.

"Want a real job?"

"Hi, Pancho. Glad to hear your voice again."

"I mean it. You've heard of You Build It, of course."

"Sure."

"They want to add an auto shop to their stores. Looking for a guy to teach them how to do it."

"I thought they only carried household supplies and tools."

"Yeah, that's now. They'll try this new idea in about fifty stores. See if it pays off."

"I could be the guy. Not sure if I want to live in the corporate world again, but I'm guessing you've already told them about me."

"Said they better grab you before someone else does. You got an appointment Thursday."

The You Build It company headquarters was only thirty minutes from the Levine home. Ed met with Andy Bryant and Ron Kaplan, the owners of the hugely successful warehouse-style chain of stores. He knew there must be hundreds of You Build Its around the country, but Linda and Ed were enjoying the freedom they now had, and the income was more than they had expected. Ed didn't need this position. But perhaps Linda did.

"We've heard good things about you," Andy said. "Talked to several people who say you're just what we need."

"Several? Glad you talked to the ones who like me."

They laughed. Ed fielded questions about his experience,

about adding this new line of products to their mix, and about his availability.

Then the owners shared some interesting information.

"We plan to retire soon," Ron said. "When we're ready, we'll sell the company, take our money, and enjoy the rest of our lives in comfort."

Ed wondered why they were telling him this.

Andy explained. "A new owner will probably bring in their own people, so we can't promise you a long-term job, but we think an auto shop will increase business and help bring a higher price when we sell."

"So, if you want the job, it's yours," Ron said.

What a relief! "That's great," Ed said. "My wife thanks you."

Where HTC had been a corporate structure with clear lines drawn between departments and divisions, You Build It was run like one big family. However, Ed found it to be a family with the same culture of backstabbing and jealousies he had lived with for twenty-five years. In a unique position and expecting this to be short-lived employment, Ed was immune to the intrigue that whirled around him. It was the right job for him at exactly the right time. The company opened twenty auto shops a year, successfully selling to the thousands of customers who already shopped at You Build It. Many of the training materials and programs Ed developed are still in use today.

You Build It was a new business model achieving rapid growth across the country, with profits exploding exponentially. Again Ed found himself in an industry where money flowed like water. Andy and Ron had such high incomes that they didn't know what to do with it all. They bought Rolls Royces, twin Ferraris, and the latest models of the hottest cars, such as Mustangs and Corvettes, each day arriving at the Atlanta headquarters in a different vehicle.

When an executive announced his engagement, Ron gave the man his own unlimited American Express card to buy his fiancée a ring. It was bigger than any diamond Ed had ever seen—then or since. And if the generous owners heard that someone needed to keep an appointment outside of Atlanta, they just said, "Take the jet."

Andy and Ron acted like kids in a candy store, and they delighted in treating everyone. They gave their employees stock options at no charge. After the company sold and later went public, people who had held on to that stock were worth millions.

You Build It grew so fast that they couldn't find enough qualified store managers. The team who opened and staffed the new locations had to make quick decisions and hire anyone who seemed like they might work out.

Ed got to know one store manager named Luigi, who had been hired straight from jail. He was an immigrant who spoke broken English and wasn't educated enough to work the math necessary to report the value of his inventory, but Luigi knew a hammer from a paint brush. He just needed an opportunity to prove himself.

Luigi turned out to be the kind of guy customers and employees loved. He ran one of the company's top stores for forty years and loved his job so much he had to be forced to retire at the age of seventy. He owned stock worth eleven million dollars. There are many employees still working just for the fun of it, with enough money to secure the future for themselves and their grown children, thanks to Ron and Andy's generosity.

Ed had fun driving the tire and auto accessory sales, and in four years when they sold the company, Andy's prediction proved true. The new owners brought in their own people.

Again, Ed was a fallout of downsizing. For the second time, he and Linda talked about retirement.

"Find a job, even part time," she said.

Ed grimaced because he had missed the five-year employment requirement to qualify for stock bonuses. That income would have provided a different future. Linda continued her logical discussion.

"We have to face it, Ed. We don't have enough money yet."

"What if I work a little, also find a hobby," Ed proposed. Her hesitation spoke the truth. "I get it, Linda. You want me to stay out of your domain."

"You have to keep busy," she said, "and build our savings, too. What if one of us gets sick?"

"You've got a point," he said. "I don't want to rattle around the house, either."

"Start calling your friends. Maybe one of them will know somebody who's got a place for you."

"I'll agree to semiretire." He took her hand, gazed into her eyes, and said, "Let's enjoy these years. Who knows how many good ones are left?"

After their loving embrace, Linda said, "But don't forget about those paychecks."

Throughout his career of extensive travel and little sleep, Ed had always focused on exercise to maintain the energy required for such demanding jobs. Now he wanted to be in shape for leisure travel and activities.

Ed wasn't in a hurry to get back to work, and for a few months, he enjoyed physical pursuits such as jogging, racquetball, and boxing. He spent lovely days on the golf course. Ed remembered being an active youngster in London's East End, walking or riding his bike great distances. These days, a parent would not allow such freedom, but compared to wartime, parents thought it was safe to roam the city.

Despite spending more time biking than sitting in school, he had been a fat child and a chubby preteen. As he progressed through puberty in Canada, Ed had grown taller, slimmed down, and discovered girls. It had been important to look his best, and he found that he enjoyed exercising and keeping a fit body. Now at the age of sixty and without an employer guaranteeing a living, Ed was thankful that he had paid attention to his health. He was energetic and expected to be physically able to work for many more years.

He took up aerobics, spinning, kickboxing, weights, and daily walks with their greyhound. He was in outstanding physical condition for a sixty-year-old, but he knew he would miss the tire industry. Ed booked an occasional speaking engagement and let it be known that he was open to employment possibilities.

NINE

Linda and Ed established a rhythm that included his out-of-town training presentations at least twice a month. Preparation and travel for these engagements kept him busy, allowing Linda the alone time she relished and supplying an acceptable income stream.

As a gregarious guy, Ed loved the energy of the crowds who spoke the same language. To keep his name and face before the people who could hire him for presentations, he continued to attend tire industry conventions, expositions, and dealer celebration events. Ed's appearances always resulted in bookings.

The Global Tire Expo held in Las Vegas each November brings together tire manufacturers, tire distributors, automobile manufacturers, car dealers, and every possible business that sells to, services, or buys from any of these. Ed had been in the industry for thirty years and made hundreds of friends and thousands of acquaintances. For him, the Expo was a family reunion.

Warm welcomes and friendly embraces met him as he wandered the aisles. "Great to see ya, Ed."

"Been meaning to call you."

"Check your schedule, and we'll bring you in. Our guys could use a kick in the pants."

He filled the calendar with engagements taking him well into 2001, gratified that so many people were glad to see him and cared that he was doing just fine. Heeding Linda's advice, however, he kept his eyes and ears open for a steadier job.

"You're looking great, Ed," A. G. Evans said. His brothers Jason and Ken joined the conversation.

A bear paw slapped him on the back, and Dick Langford said, "What's up, big guy?"

The Evans family owned a large and well-respected tire distributorship in Texas, and Dick was the vice president of sales. They were Ed's longtime friends, and he had enjoyed many dinners in their homes. While Dick flitted from customer to customer, the brothers focused on Ed, and they exchanged updates on their families.

A. G. asked a question Ed had been asking himself. "Are you busy enough these days?"

The answer was clear. "I'm busy, but not enough."

"What do you want to be doing?"

"I'd like to get back into sales." Why not? He would be visiting family and old friends.

"Why don't you come work with us?"

"Are you serious?" Ed asked, reluctant to show excitement if A. G. were only being polite.

"Totally."

They discussed the possibilities over dinner, and by dessert, Ed was the East Coast territory manager for H. Evans and Sons, LLC. Their offices were in Texas, but he would work out of his Atlanta home and answer to his buddy Dick Langford.

Instructions were explicit. "Sell as much as you can at the best margin you can. We'll cover your reasonable expenses and pay a commission. No reason to give up your speaking engagements. We'll be happy if you sell our tires while you're at it."

Couldn't be more acceptable or simple. Ed called Linda to tell her about the windfall. "You can stop worrying about depleting our savings now."

"What's that limp about?" Dick asked his new salesman.

It had been a long day for Ed. He'd spent hours on his feet walking the massive expo's aisles visiting with his newly assigned customers. He'd stood for extended periods. Ed hurt all over. His back was the worst.

"These concrete floors aren't very soft," he said, laughing. "It'll feel great to sit."

The Evans contingent met for dinner, and Ed enjoyed a vastly different evening from the corporate gatherings of his past. This was a family business, and the Evans family genuinely cared about their employees. A good salesperson often receives offers to join a competitor's company, but it was rare that an Evans representative left. They were part of the family, and that's important. The atmosphere of fun, friendship, and camaraderie ushered Ed into the fold.

After a good meal and a few glasses of wine, the back pain dulled, and he ignored the fact that this discomfort seemed to occur frequently these days.

"I'm making an appointment for you," Linda said on their nightly call. "Get through the expo. You'll see the doctor when you're back in Atlanta."

The orthopedist saw nothing on the x-rays to indicate fracture, arthritis, or osteoporosis.

"Don't forget about your age," the doctor said with a grin. "The body knows, and a week on your feet is too much. Listen to the message it's sending. Sit more often. Have those sales conversations around a table instead of standing on concrete. You're in great shape, but you can't fool your old body."

With Linda's constant but loving reminders, he took it easier...for Ed. He sometimes took an aspirin or applied a hot pad to ease the discomfort in his back. Nobody objected when he suggested getting off their feet. Ed suspected the customers were appreciative. All his old friends were aging along with him, and his aches gave them fodder for conversation before delving into serious sales discussions.

"This isn't right," Linda observed. "You're in more pain now than you were a year ago. I'm finding another doctor."

After researching in depth, as only Ed's detail-oriented wife could do, she escorted her husband to the group at Wellness for Life Hospital. Their approach made sense, with medical staff working as a team to examine the patient holistically rather than within the limits of each specialty. This philosophy allowed the team to coordinate a diagnosis and implement care to better serve the entire patient.

Ed was familiar with the team method. The Evans family had initiated quality teams in their company in the early 1990s. The involvement of all employees in improving processes and procedures had been important to the company's continued success. Those who performed a job could help the managers and owners address problems because the people doing the work knew how to fix them. As equal members working on an issue, each person was free to tell the truth and improve the process.

The application in the practice of medicine seemed brilliant, and Ed trusted the diagnosis.

"Kidney stones," they said. "You feel pain when they pass."

It was plausible but mystifying. "How do you get kidney stones?" Ed asked. "No one in my family has had them."

"You probably don't drink enough water," the doctor said. "We need to keep things moving, and when we don't, stones form."

Made sense. He did drink a lot of coffee and rarely thought to take a glass of water. Following doctor's orders, Ed increased his intake. Nothing changed. The discomfort persisted. But business was good, with both speaking bookings and tire sales, and he didn't have time to see any more doctors.

Ed made it through another year by simply expecting to be in pain and ignoring it.

The 2004 Las Vegas Tire Expo was in full swing, and Ed had an 8:00 a.m. appointment to meet his biggest customer in the Evans Company exhibit space.

But he couldn't.

Couldn't stand.

Couldn't put on his pants.

Ed dropped to the floor as carefully as possible, trying not to exacerbate the sharp pain in his back. With his slacks laid beside him, he placed the left leg opening close to his foot. Slowly, Ed moved his foot into position and held the waist band. He pulled, moving the pants up and onto his leg, and then considered how to carry out the right leg. It took an hour to finish dressing.

Ed hid the pain from his colleagues and customers and somehow made it through two more days of the expo. He headed home exhausted and determined to find out what was wrong. Linda's inquiries yielded the name of a prominent internist, and after describing her husband's agonizing condition, she was able to secure an appointment for the following week.

"You do not have kidney stones, Mr. Levine."

"Then what the hell is it?"

"Today's x-rays look like tumors in your lung. I'm ordering biopsies. Let's hope they're benign."

While the Levines waited a few days for the results of the biopsies, they discussed the previous doctors. "They were supposed to be the best," Ed lamented. "How could they get it so wrong?"

"I don't think they're the best," Linda snapped. "Wellness for Life, my ass! We should sue! Get their licenses revoked!"

A year with the wrong diagnosis had allowed tumors to grow and multiply. But the Levines hoped for the best. Benign would be good. Ed could live with that result. Literally.

Linda drove them to the Atlanta medical center to hear the biopsy report. For forty-five minutes, they didn't speak, each deep in their thoughts. She focused on negotiating the traffic while Ed thought of all the reasons the tumors could be benign. Each was hiding their fear from the other, neither successful.

Holding hands, they entered the hospital lobby and found the color-coded hallway leading to the elevator bank to the surgeon's tenth-floor office. The receptionist smiled as she checked Ed in, trying to make them feel welcome in a place no one wants to visit. After fifteen minutes, a nurse announced

Ed's name, and they followed her to an examining room.

They waited.

"I hear his voice from the hall," Linda said. "Maybe we're next."

They weren't.

"I'm getting the nurse," Ed said.

"He'll be here when he gets here," his patient wife said. "Relax."

They couldn't.

The man who had briefly met Ed before the biopsy procedure had been dispassionate. Business-like. A doctor whose chosen specialty involved unconscious patients. Surgeons must tell you the way it is rather than what you want to hear, and Ed was prepared for the worst news because the pain indicated something was terribly wrong.

The door opened, and their future briskly stepped into the room. He didn't offer a handshake or a smile as he opened the file.

"Sorry to keep you waiting," the doctor absentmindedly said as he leafed through the reports, then turned to face his patient. "Stage four lung cancer. You have just a few weeks. Get your affairs in order."

No frills. No "sorry to tell you this." A clean incision. Surgery without anesthesia. Linda and Ed were stunned silent, watching the doctor and waiting for more information.

He stood up and walked to the door. "I have to leave," the doctor said. "I'm late. My son's in a play. Call if you have any questions."

Questions? Of course, they had questions! Linda frowned and shook her head, as confused as her husband.

"Can you believe that guy?" Ed exploded. "Tells me I've got the worst kind of cancer and walks out of here like it's nothing."

"It is nothing. To him."

Ed didn't know what to do next. Update his will? Get a second opinion? The nurse returned and penetrated their fog with kindness and information. Ed would see an oncologist at a renowned institution in Atlanta and learn about options.

The drive home was intensely silent as Linda and Ed each processed the diagnosis. Stage four. Ed didn't think there was a stage five.

PART FOUR
ONE

CANCER

Ed phoned the Evans family and his boss Dick Langford and spoke to them on a conference call. "Thanks for the opportunity to work with such a fine company," he said, trying to keep his composure while explaining that he was dying.

"But why are you resigning?" A. G. asked.

"I'm not going to be able to work, of course."

Dick Langford spoke up. "I don't believe it. You'll get the treatments. For a change of pace, you can make a few phone calls. Sell a few containers of tires."

"But I have cancer. Just a few weeks left."

"Tell you what," A. G. said. "You do what you have to do, do what you want to do, and we'll keep you on the payroll."

Ed couldn't speak. He still had a job and didn't have to do anything but fight the cancer. What a blessing to be part of this company and this family.

The Levines sought more opinions. The first doctors were wrong about kidney stones. Maybe this one had made a mistake as well. They made appointments with the top oncologists in Boston and New York and prayed for a miracle.

Both confirmed the diagnosis. Ed had only a short time to live. Brokenhearted, he and Linda returned home and began to get their affairs in order before time ran out.

"I may have only a few weeks left, but I'm alive today," he said to Linda. "I'm going to fight."

Tearfully, she said, "If you can do it, I will too."

That shared determination drove the couple to journey as advocates rather than victims.

"I've fought for everything I ever accomplished," Ed said. "It's never been easy, but I've overcome. Cancer isn't going to beat me. Not yet."

They might have believed it. At the time, they only needed hope…and so far, had not found a reason for any.

Back in Atlanta, they met Oncologist Dr. Martin and learned that the protocol would be radiation to the most prolific tumor sites. The schedule began immediately.

"You should feel normal at first," Dr. Martin said, "but after the second treatment, you could begin to see effects."

"Like what?"

"Fatigue. Hair loss. Achiness. Maybe nausea."

Linda was silent, but Ed spoke to the doctor's back as he turned to the door. "Will I be able to work?"

"You can do whatever you feel like doing." And he left without another word.

Why were these cancer doctors so cold? Did dealing with death force them to avoid attachment? Linda and Ed gathered their notes and the brochures explaining radiation treatment and walked out of the examining room into their new reality.

Ed only had weeks to live. He was far too ill to think of anything else. He was in pain and scheduled daily for treatment.

The chemo and radiation took everything out of him and made him extremely sick. But the constant phone calls, e-mails, and encouragement from the Evans family and Dick Langford gave Linda and Ed great comfort in their darkest time.

The nightmare became their life. As weak and sick as Ed was, he and Linda nevertheless knew they must follow the doctor's directive to get his affairs in order. Ed updated his will, made sure all financial accounts were in Linda's name, left instructions for the funeral, including a guest list. Because there were too many tumors to pinpoint all of them, radiation was not a reliable therapy. Nevertheless, the oncologist scheduled several sessions to try every possibility. He explained that the greater chance of successfully prolonging Ed's life was chemotherapy.

They reported to the hospital for treatments. The effects were as expected.

Vomiting, cold sweats, fatigue, and weakness plagued Ed and kept his desperate wife busy attempting to ease his discomfort. "Let me help you back to bed," Linda said as she wiped her husband's face with a wet cloth. "This is the third time you've vomited in the last hour."

"I don't think I've got the energy to make it to the bathroom again," Ed said.

Linda tucked him in, placed a small plastic trash can within easy reach in anticipation of his next wave of nausea, and left him, already asleep.

Ed's humor helped them endure the weeks of agony and fear until their next appointment. "Good news, Linda. Look at this. . . the bald patches have found each other."

"Yes, that Bruce Willis look is so stylish."

"Let's hope the poison is doing its job on my tumors, too."

They expectantly returned for a follow-up visit to Dr. Martin. Most of Ed's hair was gone, and that had to be a sign that the chemo was effective. When the doctor entered their room, he glanced at them with a nod and thumbed through the file.

"We didn't expect much from radiation, as you know," he said as he indicated the charts, "and we were correct."

Linda and Ed would have been comforted if the doctor had so much as looked at them while delivering the news. He continued in a flat tone as if he were reading a grocery list. "The chemotherapy seems to be slightly effective."

At least there was a little to be happy about.

"We'll adjust your protocol and begin a new regimen in six weeks. In the meantime, maybe the chemo and radiation will continue to attack your tumors. At least the adjusted radiation should have a palliative effect and ease your pain. My scheduler will contact you to set up appointments."

He shook their hands in what the couple took to be a show of kindness and left them to absorb the fact that not much had changed since the diagnosis.

Ed had lost his hair and spent many hours over the sink or toilet giving back meals, fighting fatigue and fear, and nothing had come of it. Linda and Ed held hands as they numbly left the examining room, sure that the short time left was now significantly reduced.

In the hall, Nurse Henderson approached the Levines. "I want to tell you something," she said. "Let's take a seat in the conference room."

They were mystified but welcomed her friendly demeanor as they sat, expectantly waiting.

"I recently attended a conference in Miami Beach," she

said.

Ed thought of his stint in Florida many years before when he was a young hairdresser. Fond memories, but what did this have to do with dying of lung cancer?

"There was a presentation about a new drug."

Linda and Ed looked at each other, both hoping to learn that this would be their miracle cure. Nurse Henderson's next statement dashed any expectations.

"Trials so far have shown it to be only minimally effective to treat lung cancer."

Ed's heart sank. "Then why are you telling us about it?"

"The presentation talked about unexpected results. I think the findings might apply to you."

"Does Dr. Martin know about this?"

"He didn't attend the same session, but I'll give him the information. The drug is Iressa™. The FDA approved it in 2003 for patients with advanced non-small cell lung cancer." It was now 2005. "It seems to enhance the effects of radiation. It only helps 10 percent of the patients, but for those with a specific mutation, it seems to work."

"Do I have that mutation?"

"We don't know yet, but it's worth a shot, right?"

"I'll try anything!"

Nurse Henderson called the next day. "Dr. Martin studied the Iressa™ findings and thinks the immunotherapy drug could work for you. Come back as soon as you can, and we'll check you out."

The results showed that the tumors were still growing, but

Ed tested positive for the mutated gene and could start Iressa™ immediately.

"I'm sorry, but for now you'll have to pay for it. If it works for you and others with the mutation, the FDA will approve a new trial, and you'll be enrolled."

Tears filled Ed's eyes. "Thanks for our first glimpse of a future."

For several weeks Linda drove Ed to the hospital each day. He took the drug orally and received radiation.

Nurse Henderson had given them hope that day. Spurred by new optimism, Linda acted. With her background in medical technology and chemical research, she studied published articles, requested medical reports, and talked to specialists about the drug with the unpronounceable name. Gefitinib.

Its United States history is unique. Named Iressa™ by manufacturer AstraZeneca™, it was the first therapy targeted to specifically treat lung cancer. Following the Federal Drug Administration's standard trial protocols, AZ's findings replicated results reported in Europe and Asia. Gefitinib significantly shrank tumors in enough patients for the FDA to accelerate its process. In 2003, the FDA approved Iressa™ in the United States for the treatment of non-small cell lung cancer.

"This is confusing," she said to Ed as he dozed in his recliner. "The FDA changed its mind." Her husband listened while she explained the discouraging information.

Earlier in 2005, the agency removed the drug from the market when follow-up trials of randomly selected lung cancer patients found that Iressa™ was no more effective than standard care. Only those patients whose tumors showed shrinkage remained on the treatment. Closer analysis revealed that the drug successfully treated patients whose cancer had the

EGFR gene. Ninety countries other than the United States continued to use gefitinib to treat all lung cancer patients.

"It's gonna work for me," Ed weakly declared. "I'm not ready to die."

Linda smiled and returned to her computer. She monitored Ed's progress in hopes that he was right. After about two weeks, she said, "Do you realize what you're doing?"

Her husband was picking dead blooms off her rose bushes and laughing as their greyhound, Ben, nuzzled his hand in hopes Ed would play with him. "Yeah," Ed said absentmindedly. "Oh, I see what you mean." Without his noticing, the debilitating nausea, weakness, and fatigue had lessened.

They hugged, and Ed said a silent prayer of thanks to whatever higher power had led him to Iressa™ and perhaps normalcy. As the pain decreased, he resumed exercise and began to build back strength. Three months later, the Levines awaited the CT scan results.

Dr. Martin smiled as he pointed to the films. "Comparing the new scans to these earlier ones, we can see that all the tumors have shrunk or disappeared. Even the original lung tumors are now very small. You're a lucky guy, Ed. Iressa™ came along just in time to save your life."

"How long can I continue taking it?"

"As long as it's working for you." He reached the door, then turned and said, "You know, Ed, you have a better chance than many patients. You're in excellent physical shape. That's going to mean a lot while your body fights this disease."

Linda and Ed were speechless. Optimism from the man who was usually detached. They clung to this germ of hope.

Iressa™ proved its effectiveness in treating the EGFR mutation, and after two years, the FDA approved the new clinical trial. Ed no longer had to pay for the drug that was giving him his life back.

The Levines learned that many patients who were successfully treated with Iressa™ during the first trial had to discontinue the drug simply because their oncologists didn't complete the required paperwork. Documentation for FDA approval of the drug was necessary, and many of their friends desperately sought doctors who would comply. Their survival depended on such tenuous circumstances as the efficiency of a doctor's staff or a physician's willingness to take his staff's time for the tedious reporting.

"This doctor might be a cold fish," Ed said to Linda, "but he gave me back my life."

"And mine," said his tearful wife.

TWO

It was a miracle! Ed continued taking Iressa™ orally once a day, and though some effects took longer to ease, he resumed a somewhat normal life. His sense of humor helped him keep a positive attitude, though Linda often was not amused.

"Why are you pushing yourself so much? I don't see how you can go from vomiting over the toilet to calling your customers and joking about it."

"I am not going to surrender, Linda. I refuse to be a victim." If only the cancer would continue to cooperate.

Ed began exercising again. At first, he could use only the lightest weights and easiest machines, until repetition and effort paid off. Strength and balance improved. Ed's hard work fought the forces killing his body, but he believed that only the fighters live.

As he felt increasingly better, he worked from home. The distraction of speaking with customers kept him from focusing solely on cancer, and the income helped to replace funds spent on Iressa™.

"Hi, Antoinette. My records show that you're probably low on a few items. Give me a purchase order number, and I'll replenish your stock."

"Don't you have cancer?"

"Sure. I'm on bad drugs. Have to see my oncologist monthly…but I can write an order."

"You're amazing! Here's a big one. A truckload of tires. I expect you like those commissions to keep coming."

"Yep. It's going to be a blowout of a funeral in about thirty years. I have to pay in advance."

The Levine's credited AstraZeneca's™ belief in Iressa™ for extending Ed's life, but lung cancer took an unexpected toll. "Hi, Marcus. I'm going to be in your area next week. When can I come to your office?"

The customer hesitated so long that Ed said, "If next week doesn't work, let's find a date that does."

Marcus coughed and said, "You know, Ed, maybe we can just make it a phone call. No need to expose anyone."

"Expose anyone to what?"

"Don't you still have cancer?"

"I'm doing great, Marcus, but that's not the point." He had to risk the relationship and set this guy straight. "Cancer isn't contagious. You can't catch it from anyone else."

Silence. Then, "Sure, Ed. Why don't you give me a call in a couple of weeks?"

While exuberant that the miracle drug was working for him, Ed realized something had to be done to educate the public about the realities of cancer.

"I want to address the stigma," he told Linda. "Even leprosy has a better reputation than cancer."

"What are you thinking?"

"I'm a speaker. I motivate people. I can be a spokesperson for lung cancer."

Linda returned to research mode and discovered the Lung Cancer Crusade. "We don't have to reinvent the wheel," she reported. "The Crusade has been promoting awareness since 1995."

It was a perfect match. With the help and materials the Crusade provided, Linda and Ed enlisted doctors and patients to help establish a chapter in Georgia. Several local hospitals became involved in the effort.

Linda continued to delve into a study of cancer and gained a detailed understanding of the disease. The information was disheartening. "Did you know that lung cancer research is the least funded of all cancers? Not only that, insurance in Georgia doesn't cover treatment if it's in pill form. Only the liquid because it's administered in a hospital."

"You're talking about two separate injustices," Ed said. "Let's take one at a time. Why isn't there more research going on?"

"It's about money, of course. Not enough is raised or designated for lung cancer." They believed a cure was surely possible, and the Levines could promote the effort to develop it. Greater awareness led to more funds raised, which meant more research, resulting in improved treatments and longer life.

"Our Crusade has a lot to accomplish. Everyone can use their connections to raise money and publicize the cause. For starters, we can send speakers to every group who'll listen to us."

And they did. Devoted to their mission, Linda and Ed spoke to groups on behalf of pharmaceuticals Bayer, Pfizer, and AstraZeneca™, seeking funding and support. They drove across Georgia to conferences. Ed ran races and marathons to show the effectiveness of treatment. They spoke to organizations. Their efforts raised money and awareness, and the

Levines received valuable recognition. Magazine and news-paper articles. Television and radio interviews. The goal was simple: Stop Georgians from dying every two hours from lung cancer.

The Georgia Crusade volunteers kept busy, and more or-ganizations agreed to hear presentations. Their ranks swelled as medical staff and institutions joined, and many people who had lost loved ones helped in the fight.

Over the years, Linda and Ed granted many interviews to encourage others that you can outlive your diagnosis. Many individuals contacted them directly. Recognizing the impor-tance of maintaining physical strength, Ed counseled people to exercise despite the pain. "I'm not a coddler," Ed would say to patients straightaway. "You will die if you don't keep moving."

When patients called and needed a kick in the ass, Ed was their guy. If they wanted clinical advice, Linda was the expert. "It's a brutal battle," Ed bluntly declared. "I have no sympathy for patients who do not want to fight."

The Levines focused on state politicians to address the in-surance inequity. The Crusade was too small an organization to afford a lobbyist, but Ed and Linda nevertheless proceeded with the determination of crusaders.

"I'd like an appointment to meet with the senator, please."

"Have you spoken with the congressman representing your district?"

"No. When is the senator available?"

"Please call back after you have seen your congressman."

Okay, they would have to take baby steps.

"I'd like an appointment to meet with the congressman, please."

"Are you a resident of his district?"

"Yes."

"What is this regarding?"

Linda explained. The receptionist put her on hold. The call disconnected. Linda tried again. The receptionist was unapologetic but remembered her. "The congressman can give you ten minutes." The date was in two months.

"Thank you." Yes!

Linda and Ed drove to the state capitol building and saw their congressman as scheduled. His coiffed gray hair and commanding demeanor presented a picture that could have been titled Southern Statesman. They took their seats in front of his highly polished oak desk and made their case.

"A bill like Texas and several other states have passed could save hundreds of lives," Ed said. "It's simply a matter of requiring insurance companies to cover a drug in any of its forms, either liquid or pill. As it stands, only liquids administered intravenously in a hospital are insured, but often pills are the easiest and best treatment."

Without specifically asking, the congressman and subsequent state senators they visited indicated they were interested in contributions to their campaigns. They would sponsor legislation in return for donations.

"Our Lung Cancer Crusade can support you publicly, but we have no funds. A bill will cost the state nothing. Don't you agree that its impact will benefit you both politically and financially?"

The state politicians weren't interested. It was clear that if there was no money to give, they had no time for the cause. So, the Levines took their crusade to Washington—to Georgia

Senator Saxby Chambliss.

The senator's secretary answered the request for a meeting, and he agreed to see them when he would next be in Atlanta.

"Thank you for meeting with us, Senator Chambliss."

He gave more than the fifteen minutes his secretary had allotted as they discussed lung cancer awareness and the insurance issue. Ed and Linda left his office encouraged but with no assurances that he would help.

In the meantime, senators from several other states introduced resolutions recognizing the need for lung cancer awareness and research. To the Levines' amazement, Senator Chambliss joined the parade after all. On November 16, 2006, Linda and Ed were in the Congressional Chamber with him when Senate Resolution 620 was approved.

Resolved, That the Senate

1. *Designates November 2006 as "National Lung Cancer Awareness Month"; and*

(Reaffirms the Senate's commitment to—

(A) Advancing lung cancer research and early detection, and particularly the Lung Cancer Crusade of Georgia's goal of significantly increasing the five-year survival rate of individuals diagnosed with lung cancer in the United States to 50 percent within 10 years; and

(B) Working with all federal agencies involved in cancer research to develop a coordinated roadmap for accomplishing that goal.

Senator Chambliss congratulated them and handed them three of the most treasured documents Linda and Ed had ever received: a copy of the resolution, the Congressional Record documentation of the resolution, and a congratulatory letter signed by President George W. Bush. Overcome with emotion, they thanked him with a hearty handshake. Then, the senator turned to speak with his colleagues, indicating that time with him had ended.

The Levines hoped this recognition would gain momentum for their cause, and the subsequent local and national coverage of the resolution did result in the awareness they needed. Linda and Ed returned home to ringing phones and flowing letters.

"Mr. Levine," the woman on the line said. She began to cry.

"Yes, can I help you?"

She tried to say her name, but emotion overcame her. Ed understood. "Do you want to talk to me about lung cancer?" he asked.

"Um-hum," she managed.

"Do you live in Georgia?"

"Yes," she said, calmer now.

"We can talk now, or we can meet."

"Now." Ed heard her quietly crying.

He told her his story. The fear. The physical and emotional pain. The desperation for anything that would extend his life. The good fortune that Iressa™ was working for him. Ed couldn't count the number of patients and family members who sought his counsel and comfort, nor the volume of tears they shed together. These brave souls were as much a solace to Ed as he was to them. Sadly, not one is still alive.

The Lung Cancer Crusade work continued for six years.

Both Linda and Ed remained active as speakers, counselors, and media representatives. Magazines, newspapers, and even book references recounted their story. The Levines received awards and recognition. They never sought the limelight, but publicity helped their cause, and more contributions funded more research.

Together, Ed and Linda defiantly fought the enemy.

THREE

Thanks to AstraZeneca™, Ed had a life. At home, he continued Iressa™ with only monthly visits to the oncologist. That regimen allowed him to sell tires if he felt like it and also work for lung cancer awareness. If there had been any funds to spare, they could have traveled a bit. Thanks to the Evans Company allowing him to continue working, Ed could earn a paycheck.

During the five years prior to Iressa™ FDA approval, the Levines paid about fifty thousand dollars for the drug. It was money they didn't have. Harris Tire Company had downsized him after twenty-four and a half years, denying Ed the fully vetted pension and benefits of a thirty-year employee. Even though he never missed a day of work, and his sales numbers always came in above forecast, Ed's retirement income was a fraction of what he would have been due if the new regime hadn't gotten rid of the old guys and brought in their own team.

They lived frugally, never going to restaurants or movies. The Levines didn't care about those things, only about extending Ed's life. If he were destined to die of cancer, he vowed, he wouldn't go gently.

In 2010, things began to change. Something was going on, but he ignored the aches and discomfort and focused on living each day as well as possible.

"What's wrong?" Linda asked.

"What do you mean?"

"You're limping."

Ed had to confess. "It's my right groin area. I feel a lump. At first, it was just soreness."

The oncologist confirmed their fears and prescribed radiation to alleviate the pain while allowing the Iressa™ to shrink the tumor. Then there were more.

"Your right adrenal gland shows a growth."

"This was a quick one," Ed said. "What does that mean?"

In his typically blunt manner, Dr. Martin said, "The drug might not be working for you."

Linda and Ed could hardly process the ramifications of that remark. Was this the beginning of the end...again?

"So, what do we do?"

"We continue to watch your scans."

"But what about this new tumor? Can it be treated? Radiation maybe? Surgery?"

The oncologist looked at his patient and said, "Be realistic, Ed. You've lived several years when we thought you only had a few weeks. Let's hope the Iressa™ can overcome this and slow its growth, but be prepared for more tumors to crop up."

No way! "Is it possible to remove this one surgically?"

"Theoretically, but there are too many risks. I won't do it."

There was no more discussion with this guy. Deflated but not defeated, Linda and Ed talked about options.

"You can't blame him," she said, "even though I think he's

a coward."

"Face it, Linda. He thinks I'm going to die. Soon."

Through her tears, she said, "What do you want to do now?"

"Find a surgeon."

Linda went to the Internet. She was relentless. Only a few surgeons would speak with her, but finally, one agreed to meet.

She was prepared. "We know this is dangerous, but Ed is strong. If you don't operate, you're signing his death certificate." Her extensive research and logical arguments, with a little emotional tug added, convinced the doctor to agree.

It did not go well.

Linda informed her husband that he had been in surgery at least an hour longer than the doctor had anticipated. "He seemed very concerned when he finally met with me," she said. "It wasn't as simple as he expected."

She took Ed home to recuperate. For a week, he endured weakness and nausea, exacerbated by the discomfort of a drainage tube in his abdomen. They returned to the doctor's office to remove the tube. He predicted that the symptoms would soon improve, and Ed could begin to heal.

Instead, Ed began to sweat profusely while still in the doctor's office. Then he descended into blackness.

He regained consciousness in the emergency room of the adjoining hospital where he was admitted. The doctor had nicked his pancreas during surgery, causing pancreatitis. Ed suffered excruciating upper abdominal pain radiating into his back. Because eating anything, especially foods high in fat, led to nausea and vomiting, he was fed intravenously. Ed remained in the hospital for three weeks and then at home on medication for several months. It was a setback, but removing the tumor gave him another two years of life.

Until a growth developed in his abdomen.

Linda, ever the advocate for her husband, spoke up. "Please scan Ed's pelvis," she said during a routine appointment. "He's acting like he's experiencing discomfort in that area."

"I didn't think you noticed," Ed said. He was so determined to carry on as if he were well despite the cancer in his body that he didn't think to mention this change.

The scan revealed a bladder tumor. A urologist was added to the litany of doctors who cared for Ed.

"We have no choice. I'll start you on chemo to reduce the tumor so I can remove it. If we're lucky, there'll be no more growth."

It was troubling that more tumors seemed to be appearing. Every three months after each cystoscope, the Levines prayed that the chemo and Iressa™ were working. When the results showed no more growths and enough shrinkage in the original tumor, the doctor operated.

The best result of having bladder cancer was finding Dr. Pravin. This rare practitioner had a sincere and caring manner with patients, who were scared for their lives and grasping for hope. Thanks to his diligence, Ed survived. The Levines had beaten the odds once again.

In 2011, new growths appeared, and the oncologist reported frightening news. "The Iressa™ seems to have lost its effectiveness for you. After all, you've been on it for seven years. We can continue it for a short while and, in the meantime, try to find another drug that might work."

This could be Ed's death warrant. As usual, Linda scoured the Internet for alternatives.

"We're going to the Dana-Farber Cancer Institute," she announced. "It's time for another opinion."

In Boston, they saw an oncologist who specialized in Ed's genetic mutation. "Stop the Iressa™ for a month or two and restart it. Maybe your body needs to reboot."

To everyone's surprise, that's exactly what happened. After three months, Ed resumed taking Iressa™. The miracle drug performed more miracles. The metastasis seemed to be under control, though to eliminate some of the possible tumor sites, the Atlanta oncologist removed all the lymph nodes from Ed's right pelvis and groin. The resulting lymphedema left him battling swelling, tightness, restricted range of motion, and occasional infections. Nevertheless, he worked to maintain strength and diligently continued exercising and walking their dog.

Linda and Ed used the gift of his extended life to again focus on promoting lung cancer awareness. Their mission also publicized his unique longevity, and one day, Ed received an unexpected phone call.

"Mr. Levine, this is Dr. Bronstein. Would you be willing to participate in a clinical trial?"

An oncologist at Massachusetts General Research Institute, this doctor knew more about Iressa™ than anyone else and shared his knowledge throughout the medical world.

"We would like to study your tumor cells and learn from you."

"Of course."

Again, the Levines went to Boston and another world-renowned institution. Sadly, the effort to grow Ed's cells in mice failed, and nothing came of this research.

Iressa™ saved Ed for a total of twelve years. Until it didn't.

FOUR

Iressa™ had run its course, and they were desperate to find another miracle drug. Linda scoured every resource for information and succeeded in enrolling her husband in new clinical trials.

The experimental drugs did not stop the cancer from spreading, and in fact, the effects of one caused Ed to be hospitalized after developing a neutropenic fever with each dose. The resulting low red and white blood cell and platelet counts put him at risk for infection or death. He received high doses of antibiotics as well as blood transfusions.

Ed's pain management and comfort consumed the couple, who all the while hoped for his admission to more clinical trials.

Then the cancer spread to his abdomen, causing Ed tremendous pain. They were desperate. Linda found another trial that would accept him until scans revealed numerous tumors affecting his kidneys.

"In addition to the tumors blocking kidney drainage, your creatinine is too high," the doctor said. "You don't qualify for this trial."

"What are our options?"

"A stent would allow urine to drain. That could make the difference."

As always, Ed was willing to try anything. They waited for the stent to be inserted and then thankfully began infusions of Keytruda™, one of the new immunotherapy treatments. Keytruda™ works to boost the body's natural defense against disease: the immune system. The drug's publicity states that Keytruda™ blocks the Programmed Death Receptor-1 pathway, preventing cancer cells from hiding from the T cells, which detect and fight infections and diseases. This was just what Ed needed to stop the spread of the monster destroying his body, but the risks were daunting. Any time during treatment or even after it ceased, Merck's drug could cause the immune system to attack normal organs and tissues.

No matter. Keytruda™ was his only hope.

Even with the drug, symptoms worsened. Ed was always cold. His muscles grew stiffer, and it was hard to do anything but languish in the recliner.

He was soon due for the second Keytruda™ dose when one afternoon, Ed realized that his entire right side was paralyzed. Linda called the only doctor who had showed compassion.

She managed to speak despite her fear. "So sorry to bother you, Dr. Pravin, but we don't know what to do. Ed is paralyzed!"

"Go to the ER immediately," he said, not bothering to determine if this involved his specialty. "I'll meet you there." This saint of a man admitted Ed to the hospital and ordered an extensive battery of tests. After several days and many specialists, they received the shocking diagnosis.

"The lung cancer has metastasized to your brain." The news was devastating, leaving Ed speechless. Linda asked questions and heard that there was hope.

"The tumor is operable, with risks, of course."

"I'll try anything," Ed said. "When can we do it?"

Ed has little memory of the two weeks following surgery. Linda moved into her husband's hospital room and made sure everything possible was done to care for him. Her cool touch and loving smile comforted him as Ed drifted from dreamy wakefulness to sleepy awareness of the activity around him.

"I see you and your ugly face!" Perspiring, Ed fought his covers. "You can't take me!" he protested to his nightmare. "Go to hell!"

For days Ed attacked the monster, yelled and swore. "That son of a bitch left me his message," Ed said to Linda, "but Satan didn't know he was up against Ed Levine." With a weak grin he declared, "He hasn't gotten me yet."

The tumor had been in the left frontal lobe, affecting the entire right side of his body, as well as memory and speech. His right side was now useless, and the left was partially paralyzed as well. There was no way Linda could care for him at home, so he would first be transferred to a rehabilitation facility.

The anticipation of Ed's eventual homecoming frightened both Ed and Linda, neither knowing how to prepare their house for his special needs. A call from her younger brother was a godsend. She hung up the phone and tearfully said, "Edwin is coming Saturday."

Ed cried, too. "Thank God." They had not seen him in years.

The oldest of six children, Linda's position in the birth order gave her status along with responsibility. The Pearsons are a staid family, undemonstrative in their affection. Over the years, they and the Levines had never spent much time visiting each other. Linda's personality, whether a result of nature or nurture, developed into introversion, self-sufficiency, tenacity, and love of detail. These traits saved her husband's life. But now she needed help.

Ed had no illusions. His first wife, Marsha, had successfully alienated their children from him, and though they knew about their father's cancer, he never heard from them. Linda and Ed had only one possibility of help.

Edwin, Linda's middle sibling, drove from Florida and moved in. "You're in a hell of a state, Ed."

The patient tried to say, "Don't be so encouraging," but couldn't get it out.

"Didn't mean to make you guys cry."

"You're a lifesaver," Linda said.

"Glad I can help out. Sorry, it's been so long. Been busy." They all knew that was true. Edwin had first had to make sure their elderly mother would be okay alone in Florida. Edwin was the only one who helped her with everything, including doctors and hospitals.

Ed's brother-in-law is a man of few words, a fact that contributed to two divorces. He simply shrugged and got to work. Edwin did all the heavy lifting, literally, and he puttered. He didn't ask for directions; he saw what needed to be done for his family and did it. Edwin quietly roamed the house and property, repairing any and every item that needed fixing or replacing, and even some that didn't.

He built a ramp at the back door, so when Ed came home from the hospital, they could get the wheelchair into the house. He made everything handicapped accessible. When he had to go back to Florida, he took the large dog with him, so Linda could be unrestricted in tending her patient at the hospital and completing all the other tasks she needed to do. He brought the greyhound back after Ed returned home. Edwin did everything to make their lives easier, and Ed will never forget that he was the only family member who cared to help.

They called it a rehabilitation hospital. Ed called it a travesty. Were there no inspections? No management oversight of cleanliness and staff? No oversight of management? The physical therapists were excellent, and that fact is a miracle because all other therapists and staff were incompetent, careless, disinterested, and sometimes cruel.

Most of the nurses were from Africa and didn't speak English. With Ed's garbled speech, it was impossible to communicate verbally with them.

"I can't reach the tray," he said as best he could.

The nurse ignored him. Perhaps she didn't understand.

"Here," he said, motioning to himself. "Eat here." Ed mimed feeding himself.

She left the room. It would be hours before she or anyone else returned. The breakfast tray always remained on the far table, safely out of Ed's reach, growing colder, never to be eaten. Driving from home two hours each way, Linda would arrive later with decent food for her husband.

Despite his poor circumstances, Ed was in better condition than the old man in the opposite bed. Paralyzed and mute, the man had to be harnessed, hoisted up, moved along a rail hung from the ceiling, and then lowered into a wheelchair. Several times he was hoisted with full diapers and left hanging for hours. Ed tried to call for help, but his requests were ignored.

Regularly, at 5:00 a.m., a nurse came into the room to dress Ed for physical therapy. Four hours later, she wheeled him to the appointment.

"Can't you let me sleep longer?" he managed to ask when an English-speaking person checked on him.

The answer was aggravating. "We are very busy. We have a schedule, you see."

Their schedule did not include bathing. Once, it was an entire week between showers. Thankfully, it was not the week of the transfusion from hell.

The nurse was trying. Ed could tell that as she bit her lip, squinted in intensity, and tapped his arm in search of a site. She uttered a slight grunt with each jab of the needle. So did Ed. Again and again she tried until the blood that would never flow from Ed's veins into the needle covered him and the bed. Thankfully, her replacement did a better job of it. One can only hope that nurse number one received further training before torturing another patient.

Linda took total care of her husband from 11:00 a.m. to 8:00 p.m. each day and ensured he was brought to each therapy appointment. Exercising was hard work, but Ed would not accept paralysis or speech impairment. He also would not accept incompetent therapists. Several lacked skills, and some were simply unsuited for a vocation requiring compassion and intelligence.

A few were too young to relate to him. Their computer-generated exercises and puzzles required responses a sixty-plus-year-old Cockney couldn't answer correctly. He had trouble thinking logically, remembering details, and constructing sentences. He quickly became frustrated, and the young therapists did the same.

Ed was determined to walk again. His hands and arms would once more do his bidding. He would learn to think, to speak clearly. No question about it.

"Don't expect too much," the rehab staff warned.

"Don't tell me what to expect," he told the young, incompetent kids who called themselves therapists. Ed Levine set them straight. "I'll walk, I'll talk, I'll wax my cars. That's a promise."

Ed heard the word can't, and that challenge ensured that he would make it happen.

His progress brought attention from doctors, who had not expected success. He granted the surgeon permission to use his brain tumor for research. An examination reported that the Keytruda™ seemed to be effective, and the stent allowing the kidneys to drain kept the creatinine low enough for him to continue the trial. Thus, the first stop upon leaving the rehabilitation hospital was to the clinic for another infusion. Though Keytruda™, as of now, has yet to be FDA approved for Ed's particular lung cancer mutation, the infusions continue to this day.

Linda put the hospital bed in the living room so that her husband could stay downstairs. It was months before he saw their second-floor bedroom. Still paralyzed on the right side and partially on the left, Ed was able to speak but little else. Linda's small stature made her physically unable to transfer him from bed to wheelchair, to shower, or to toilet. Thankfully, Edwin returned to supply the unselfish help they needed, staying until the couple could manage without him. Their greyhound returned with Edwin and had missed his family as much as they missed him. His companionship was, again, a great comfort.

Home health aides and therapists came to Ed for six months. Physical, occupational, speech. Between visits and after insurance no longer paid for home therapy, Linda worked with him, repeating the exercises until both were exhausted. Linda and Edwin took Ed to monthly immunotherapy and periodic oncologist appointments. The doctors expressed amazement at his improvement.

"I promised I would walk again. Learn to speak clearly. Use my hands and arms."

"Everyone says that, Ed, but few gain proficiencies to match yours."

"The first therapists shouldn't have told me I couldn't."

Ed and Linda both dreaded and looked forward to oncologist visits, hoping to gain solutions to his lack of progress. The doctor listened to Linda's description of Ed's increasing deterioration and significant side effects.

He was blunt. "The drug is either losing its effectiveness, or it's killing you."

"I'll die without it."

"The trial guidelines are specific, Ed. The pharmaceutical company will only supply patients who are improving. I can't continue your infusions."

Ed did not get through this life by doing what other people told him to do. Or not to do. He stood up from the examination table, reached for his shirt, and informed the doctor of the facts.

"I'm going to the lab for my immunotherapy, doc. See you in three weeks." And Ed took his astonished sweetheart's hand and led Linda to the infusion suite, where the staff administered the drug to the salesman who knows how to close on the order.

EPILOGUE

October 2019

Determination and just plain cussedness brought Ed back to a functional physical condition, though pain and increasing debilitation are his chronic companions. Beginning with the brain tumor in June 2016, the constant life-saving factors have been kidney stents and immunotherapy infusions. The uncomfortable and often painful stent has been replaced twice. Now, one kidney is totally nonfunctional, and since the stent serves no purpose, he will undergo a procedure to remove it.

The immunotherapy causes severe fatigue and weakness and has destroyed Ed's thyroid gland. Its side effects make each day miserable, but without Keytruda™, his life would be over.

Despite—and in defiance of—their difficulties, Ed and his aging dog take their walk every day. It's hard work to fight when your body inexorably takes your faculties and functionality from you.

He must drink at least seventy-five ounces of water a day and is on a low potassium diet to help his remaining kidney. That means no bananas, dairy, potatoes, or tomatoes, to mention but a few things. The regimen works, but it eliminates much that he loves. Due to his early banana experience, however, that loss is tolerable.

A typical daily schedule is not very exciting.

Ed gets up at 6:30 a.m. It takes at least ninety minutes to

dress. The hardest part is putting a high-compression stocking on his right thigh, followed by a shoe on his right foot. Without help, that can take as long as thirty minutes. His useless right leg is a dead weight, compelling Ed to use both hands to lift and guide it. He has a three-foot metal implement to push the foot into the shoe, then a short shoehorn and his fingers pull out the back of the shoe. The best method to do this arduous task is to sit on the bottom hallway steps. He has the stair railing to hold on to, the floor to help him push, and the seat height to place him in the most helpful position.

Once that's done, Ed takes medications and drinks at least twenty-five ounces of water. He fills the bird feeders and puts them on the deck, then gets the dog ready for a one-hour walk. They don't go as far as they used to. Nevertheless, they keep moving for one hour. Ed doesn't know how long he will be able to continue; he's had to give up all other walks. It's getting more difficult, and he's tripping a lot. Can't take the chance of falling.

Back at home, he feeds the dog, then makes his breakfast of toast and cereal. By the time he's done, it's at least noon, and he's unable to walk anymore or do anything at all. For the rest of the day, Ed sits in a recliner with his feet elevated. Though this is what he's supposed to do, the fact is that he has no energy for any activity other than recuperating from the morning.

Many of Ed's days are spent at the hospital. The trip takes about two hours each way, and since he can no longer drive, the burden is on Linda. He usually spends a full day there, especially when he receives Keytruda™ infusions every three weeks. The immunotherapy wipes him out for a few days, and he is too tired and nauseous to do anything but rest in a recliner with the television for company. Once a week he goes to physical therapy. The balance of hospital visits involves seeing different 'ologists or undergoing MRIs and other scans.

If Ed goes anywhere with Linda, he usually sits and waits in the car because it takes too long to get out and back in. It also takes too much out of him.

At about 11:30 p.m., after the television news, he makes his tedious way upstairs. He's in bed after midnight because he must first put on a night-time leg garment that goes up to the waist. It looks like an over-padded oven mitt.

Ed now suffers seizures that affect his entire right side. His right leg collapses at the knee. His right shoulder to the elbow becomes weak and uncontrollable. His right arm sometimes shakes, and on its own, progressively reaches over his head and arches down his back. The pain worsens the farther over and behind the head it goes. Linda must hold Ed's arm down, and sometimes it takes two people to keep it from lifting over his head. Usually, about ten minutes after the seizure ceases, Ed loses all control of the arm. It just hangs limp, like it doesn't belong to anyone, and this lasts about an hour to ninety minutes. The neurologist recently prescribed medication that appears to have stopped the seizures but not the weakness or disability.

He's begun to lose his balance. If Linda knew, she would be upset and frightened. Ed can't hide his deterioration, though, and she's a smart girl. Occasionally he does fall. Recently, he collapsed while walking out of the bathroom. He couldn't get up. In the past, Linda has had to call for help, but the last time she was able to help on her own. Ed dreads the next time.

The restrictions are frustrating for Ed and miserable for Linda, even though she tries to conceal her distress. She hasn't heard from four of her five siblings in years, nor does Ed see or hear from his son and daughter. Thankfully, Linda's brother Edwin drives up from Florida twice a year. It's hard for him to make it more often because he still cares for their ninety-year-old mother. But since Ed's diagnosis, the H. Evans's family and their sales vice president have been his constant supporters and cheerleaders. Linda and Ed cherish their friendship and involvement in their lives.

Ed has reduced his focus to staying alive and not getting any worse. It aggravates him to no end because he wants to get up and do things but physically can't. As recently as last summer, even though he was restricted, he tried to be more active. Ed waxed the car. It would take a week, but he did it, just to prove that he could. Now he can't. He tinkered in the basement. Now he can't. Ed and Linda no longer take leisurely drives because he can't sit in the car for long unless he must go to the hospital for tests, treatments, or doctor visits.

Linda focuses on Ed. She refuses to visit her mother or attend social or cultural events. Her passion is making sure her husband survives one more day.

Ed's treatments continue, even as his challenges increase.

Each day is a gift. Thanks to Linda's loving advocacy and his determination, Ed has received many more days than expected, though he suspects the end of his journey is near. A life that is here today could very well end tomorrow, but a patient can keep a positive attitude and proactively pursue treatment. Ed Levine knows something about that.

One must wonder why or how he survived Nazi bombs. Poverty. Cancer. Or lifelong overt anti-Semitism. The answers, if there be answers, are simple. He chose to fight. Despite being a dummy, Ed has never given up. He never allowed circumstances to stop him from achieving his goals. From being a success. From surviving.

Ed hopes his story will encourage others to fight until there's nothing left to do.

That's what he did.

And Ed Levine is still fighting.

ACKNOWLEDGEMENTS

Sincere thanks to the following: My readers for their constructive comments: Ronnie, Armin and Maxine; The Wednesday group: Pam, Warren, Jean, and Joann; The Thursday group: Jean, Margo, Mandy, Karen, and Steve. Charles and Sally for their extraordinary effort in my behalf. The professionals who gave of themselves as mentors and coaches: Saralyn Richards, Roger Leslie, and Erin Liles. And to everyone who expressed interest in my work, I thank you for encouraging my determination to bring Ed's message to the universe.

Ronarose Chafetz Train

AUTHOR

 I always loved to write but had never felt compelled to do so until 1995 at the age of 52.

While working at a trade show in Hanover, Germany, I conversed with the security guard of the neighboring exhibit. We talked about our families, life in his country after World War II, and the Germany of today. This Memphis girl never expected to have such a fascinating and unique experience, and I wanted to remember every detail. I secured paper and began my first of many journals.

If it happens, I write it. If I contemplate it, I write it. If I find a willing reader, I am honored to share my passion. Through seminars, classes, and critique groups I continue to learn and make new and interesting friends.

My first manuscript began as a one-page assignment for my creative writing class. *Legacy* is still a work in progress, a tale of family rivalry, domestic abuse, mystery, and love. My protagonist and her story have grown in depth and complexity along with the author who created them.

I believe that it's never too late to follow your dream. I'm doing it.